A HEART FOR CREATION

A HEART FOR CREATION

Worship resources and reflections on the environment

Chris Polhill

WILD GOOSE PUBLICATIONS

First published 2010 by
Wild Goose Publications
Fourth Floor, Savoy House, 140 Sauchiehall Street, Glasgow G2 3DH, UK
Wild Goose Publications is the publishing division of The Iona Community
Scottish Charity No. SC003794 Limited Company Reg. No. SC096243

ISBN: 978-1-905010-67-7

The publishers gratefully acknowledge the support of the Drummond Trust,
3 Pitt Terrace, Stirling FK8 2EY in producing this book.

A catalogue record for this book is available from the British Library.

Overseas distribution:
Australia: Willow Connection Pty Ltd, Unit 4A, 3-9 Kenneth Road, Manly Vale, NSW 2093
New Zealand: Pleroma, Higginson Street, Otane 4170, Central Hawkes Bay
Canada: Novalis/Bayard Publishing & Distribution, 10 Lower Spadina Ave., Suite 400,
Toronto, Ontario M5V 2Z2

Printed by Bell & Bain, Thornliebank, Glasgow, UK

Mixed Sources
Product group from well-managed
forests and other controlled sources
www.fsc.org Cert no. TT-COC-002769
FSC © 1996 Forest Stewardship Council

GENERAL CONTENTS

CONTENTS IN DETAIL

Key to symbols	
✝	Prayer
♌	Liturgy
♫	Song
☒	Story
☻	Script
⊞	Reflection
✻	Poem
⚑	Creed
((◉))	Responses
☊	Action
൭	Reading

The struggle to change

The struggle to change: Liturgical resources

Key to symbols
✝ Prayer
☿ Liturgy
♫ Song
🐚 Story
😀 Script
▦ Reflection
🦋 Poem
⛏ Creed
((◎)) Responses
🚲 Action
〰 Reading

Transformation

Transformation: Liturgical resources

Appendix

Key to symbols	
✟	Prayer
🜅	Liturgy
♫	Song
🖎	Story
😊	Script
🏛	Reflection
🌠	Poem
💪	Creed
((◎))	Responses
🚲	Action
Ͼ	Reading

This book is dedicated to
my grandchildren
and the children they may one day have.

INTRODUCTION

This book is offered as a space for reflection on the environmental challenges that face us now and which will confront us in the years to come, and as a resource for preparing worship with an environmental theme. There are five sections to the book, which express aspects of the Christian spiritual journey, each beginning with a theological reflection.

We start by celebrating the amazing wonders of the universe we are part of. This is not just because it is good to praise and be thankful, but also because we will make better decisions from love of the world, rather than from fear of catastrophe. Next comes lamentation for the damage to the planet and the loss of species. This will enable true sorrow before God: this will release us from the paralysis of fear or guilt that prevents action.

The third section, Action for change, includes a six-week challenge of daily facts, actions and reflections, appropriate for Lent, with additional material for Holy Week, but suitable for any six-session programme. Some further liturgical resources complete this section.

The fourth section, Struggle to change, reflects on the difficulties we face, and on how the way of the cross can sustain and help us. And the final section, Transformation, corresponds to the Christian belief in resurrection and new life, revealing that there will be good surprises to come from the changes that we make.

As well as the usual elements of worship, there are reflections and stories that demonstrate how people are already bringing, or trying to bring, about change, and thinking about the issues.

Thank you to everyone who has shared their thoughts and stories and wrestled with ways to express them prayerfully. It is my belief that prayer changes us, and I hope that these resources will aid our prayer so that we truly reflect God's heart for creation.

Thank you also to Neil and everyone at Wild Goose Publications for their encouragement and patient attention to detail; and thank you to Pat, Sylvia, Stephanie and Brian, who read the first draft and made helpful suggestions.

Gracious God,
share with us
your heart for creation.
That we may cherish all life,

working together to heal
the damage we have done.
Knowing that in all our struggles
you are beside us,
to inspire, strengthen
and transform us.

Chris Polhill

CELEBRATING CREATION

CELEBRATION AWAKENS LOVE AND CARE

The blue haze stretched to the hedges and into the wood beyond; there was a delicate scent in the air. The other children were already into this blue space with shrieks of delight. I stood quite still, breathless and amazed, aged 8, at my first sight of bluebells – then I too was among them, busy picking a bunch for my mum, as we could back then. I grew up in the East End of London, amid crowded mean architecture and bombsites, but three times a year, on bank holiday Mondays, the church organised an outing for a hike in the Kent countryside. It was a brilliant part of the ministry and encouraged the awe I still have for the sheer beauty and immensity of creation. We celebrated the greenness, the space and the beauty of it all with our joy, and by taking a little bit back home to share.

Many who have given up on church, except to mark the milestones in life, will talk of being aware of something other than themselves, when they see a sunset; stare at the sea; gaze at mountains; walk the dog through the local park. Some will speak of finding it easier to pray or to encounter God when in the countryside. This is not a new experience. The Old Testament, from the creation stories on, has a continual theme of the goodness and glory of creation and how God is recognised there. Jesus uses nature images to teach about God and our relationship with him. Eriugena, a 9th-century Irish theologian, teaches of Christ having two shoes, one, creation, the other the Bible. The stories of the Celtic saints are strewn with accounts of their closeness to animals and the natural world, their desire to see more of it, and the conviction that to know God they must understand creation. The Franciscans carried this further and saw nature as related to us in the familial closeness of brother and sister; the Jesuits end the Ignatian exercises with the desire to find God in all things. Awe and wonder are a spiritual response to the beauty and intricacy of creation, and therefore to the Creator. It is a response that leads us to love and delight in the world about us, and therefore to celebrate this amazing universe.

It is my conviction that as we love and celebrate the natural world, of which we are a part, we will care for it as an expression of that love. So often, climate change and the consequences of global warming are presented in ways that only inspire fear and denial. It is true that humans will act out of fear to protect an environment that they need, but fear does not always inspire our best actions as a species. The interconnectedness of all things is confusing enough when we try to bring about change, without the inevitable mistakes from fearful reactions. Greed is an even poorer guide as it is concerned only with the self, and we are already aware that natural disasters affect the poorest peoples most. If we come to the difficulties presented by the environmental problems that beset us from the perspective of love and care, we are more likely to make choices that benefit the needs of our planet at this time and reflect the will of the Creator. 'God is love, and love comes from God.' St John in his first epistle is very sure of that (1 John 4:7).

To love creation is also to acknowledge its infinite goodness and blessing. Here we are on God's beautiful planet, with air to breathe; water to drink, wash and play in; food in great variety and abundance; herbs that heal; materials for homes and clothes – and a vast array of wonders to encounter and marvel at. From amazing intricate detail in the tiniest flower to an endless view of mountaintops, creation is stunning. So it is hard to understand how some of our Christian forebears developed a strain of thinking that saw this world as bad and to be shunned, full of sin and temptation. It is not the fault of the natural world if we are greedy or if we abuse it; human sin is the tragic consequence of our wrong choices. Volcanoes, tsunamis and other natural upheavals will disturb, even end our lives if we are in their path, but they are part of the way the world is made in order for it to be as it is. Creation of itself is full of blessing, a great goodness that enriches us, body, mind and spirit. Matthew Fox talks of there being millions of years of original blessing, before ever there was original sin, and that we forget that at great cost to our well-being.

It is also true that if we loved creation enough to notice the needs of the planet itself, to be aware of the variables that affect the way we live, we would be more likely to live in harmony with creation than try to dominate it. Naturally we will make spaces for ourselves to live in, but if we barrier the sea, or reroute a river, or use any other of the ways we try to contain nature, we should not be surprised if we suffer floods or other troubles. Our world is not static, but moves and changes. On the east coast of England, some salt marshes are being re-created to accommodate the natural tilt of the UK which causes our coastline to change. The biodiversity that is being reclaimed through this is fascinating, but it is hard for populations that used to live there. The kind of co-operation we need is costly and will demand all the Christian qualities of love, patience, consideration for others, sharing and service. The same is true for the way we grow and gather food. To strip the seas of fish and demand so much growth that we ruin the fertility of the land is the way of domination and greed, and also the way to hunger. It is a way that damages the intricate connectedness of sea creatures, and of plant and animal life. To live in co-operation with all of creation is the way of love and care. It would be a blessing to all life, not just our own. This is not an easy way; it will require us to grow as disciples, to struggle both within and without, and to seek that transformation that God alone can bring. I suggest, however, that it is the best way. So to love, and therefore celebrate creation involves us in the whole of the Christian journey.

Celebration, that natural human way of honouring something or someone special, is given first place in this book because it is the best place to start. Through celebration we praise God, and give thanks for the wonderful gift of life – from quarks dancing their Trinitarian dance unseen, to the planets circling the sun. We join our voices to the song of creation that praises the Maker (Psalm 148), singing with the mountains and hills and clapping our hands with the trees (Isaiah 55). We can praise the greatness of God with even more wonder than Psalm 104 because we have learned more of the intricacies of creation. As we celebrate, we express the love for creation that is a natural part of love for God the Creator. Together we celebrate, and together we become a force for change.

Chris Polhill

CELEBRATING CREATION:
LITURGICAL RESOURCES

PRAISE FOR CREATION

The world around us is full of beauty:
WE PRAISE YOUR NAME, O GOD.

For the gift of life on earth:
WE PRAISE YOUR NAME, O GOD.

Open our eyes to see your artistry,
YOUR IMAGE IN ALL THAT YOU HAVE MADE.

Where our praise is short or silent:
ALL CREATION SINGS OUT WITH JOY.

Here we join creation's song:
WE PRAISE YOUR NAME, O GOD.

God, our Creator,
we come together
to celebrate your creation:
the bright beauty about us,
the abundance of your providing;
accept this offering of praise
as we worship you,
the Maker of all.
AMEN

Chris Polhill

LIGHT UP THE WORLD

Loving God,
by whose great generosity
we are granted the gift of life,
so breathe on the spark
of your presence within us,
that we burn with a flame of love
that banishes our fear,
and lights up the world around us.

We ask this in the name of Jesus,
Light and life of the world.

John Polhill

GOD LAID THE EARTH'S FOUNDATION

When we consider the awesome works of God,
we know that we have sinned.

HOW CAN A MORTAL BE RIGHTEOUS BEFORE YOU, O GOD?
YOU LAID THE EARTH'S FOUNDATION;
YOU FIXED LIMITS FOR THE SEA;
YOU GIVE ORDERS TO THE MORNING;
YOU TIP OVER THE WATER JARS OF THE HEAVENS;
YOU HUNT THE PREY FOR THE LIONESS;
YOU KNOW WHERE THE MOUNTAIN GOAT GIVES BIRTH;
THE EAGLE TAKES FLIGHT BY YOUR WISDOM.
YOU CAN DO ALL THINGS:
NO PLAN OF YOURS CAN BE THWARTED.
WE HAVE SPOKEN OF THINGS WE DO NOT UNDERSTAND:
THEREFORE WE REPENT IN DUST AND ASHES.

'Fear not,' says the Lord, 'for I have redeemed you:
I have summoned you by name: you are mine.'

Eleanor Harris

LOST FOR WORDS

We sense your presence, O God,
in the world around us,
in the wonder and gift of this life.

You overwhelm minds and hearts.
The vastness of the universe
makes us ponder our place and part in things.
The experience of being, of living and dying,

confronts us with our mortality
and gives us glimpses of the eternal.
And it leaves us lost for words, helpless.

You delight our senses:
the rainbow's playful light, the vibrant colour of spring flowers;
the tang of the salt-sea air and the smell of freshly baked bread;
the taste of strawberries and raspberries and vanilla ice cream;
the sound of children laughing, of church bells and Bach;
the reflex grip of a tiny baby and the familiar embrace of a friend ...
And it leaves us lost for words, helpless.

Generous God, you give us so much.
But we are the people of much knowledge who lack wisdom;
the people of great power who cannot tread gently amongst living things;
the people of many possessions who crave even more;
the people of pleasures who search for contentment;
the people of ideals who slump into apathy;
the people of optimism whose hope is fragile;
the people of belief who lack faith;
the people of faith who have lost a sense of grace.
And it leaves us lost for words, helpless.

O God of grace, you are our help.
You made us to sense your presence,
delight in your creation and know your love.
Your love is faithful,
your forgiveness limitless,
your compassion endless,
more than we deserve or could ever earn.
And it leaves us lost for words, except to say ... Amen

Peter Macdonald

MADE IN GOD'S IMAGE

You have given us eyes ...
BUT WE HAVE NOT ALWAYS LOOKED AT CREATION'S BEAUTY.

You have given us ears ...
BUT WE HAVE NOT ALWAYS LISTENED TO NATURE'S SPEAKING.

You have given us tongues ...
BUT WE HAVE NOT ALWAYS JOINED EARTH'S SONG OF PRAISE.

You have given us hands ...
BUT WE HAVE NOT ALWAYS BEEN MAKERS AND MENDERS.

You have given us feet ...
BUT WE HAVE NOT ALWAYS SHARED IN THE DANCE OF LIFE.

You have given us minds ...
BUT WE HAVE NOT ALWAYS THOUGHT BEYOND OURSELVES.

You have given us wills ...
BUT WE HAVE NOT ALWAYS CHOSEN THE GOOD.

You have given us hearts ...
BUT WE HAVE NOT ALWAYS LOVED WITHOUT RESERVE.

You have made us in your image ...
FORGIVE US THAT WE DO NOT ALWAYS DISPLAY YOUR LIKENESS.

Pat Bennett

GOD COLOURS THE RAINBOW

Adapted from the Book of Job

ALL: ALL PRAISE TO GOD
        WHO COLOURS THE RAINBOW'S RIBBONS.

A: The Lord laid the earth's foundations,
        he measured it and shaped it.

B: As he set the cornerstone in place,
        the morning stars sang for joy.

A: He gave birth to the sea,
        and set its limits for ebb and flow.

B: He shook down the snow,
        and poured out the rain.

A: He let loose the lightning,
        and thundered abroad the storm.

B: He gave the earth its seasons,
        its growing time and harvests.

A: He made all that runs and crawls,
        all that swims and flies he shaped.

B: With love he made the light,
        with laughter he burnished the sun.

ALL: ALL PRAISE TO GOD
        WHO COLOURS THE RAINBOW'S RIBBONS.

Julia Morris

A VERSION OF PSALM 8

ALL: WONDERFUL CREATOR,
        THE UNIVERSE DEMONSTRATES YOUR GREATNESS.

A: The scale of creation is beyond our comprehension,
        yet babies and children wonder at its detail.

B: Creation is ordered by you;
       there is no power beyond your control.

A: When we look at the stars set in the night sky,
       even the moon, where humans have set foot,

B: we know we are insignificant,
       and wonder that you care for us individually.

A: Yet, you have given us the power to investigate our surroundings,
       and learn a little of how matter is formed.

B: You have offered us shared responsibility
       for other living creatures, for plants,
       for preserving the beauty of landscape,

A: and to work with us to complete your creation
       here on earth.

ALL: WONDERFUL CREATOR,
       THE UNIVERSE DEMONSTRATES YOUR GREATNESS.

John Polhill

PRAYER OF PRAISE
Based on Psalm 148

A: Praise the Lord from the heavens!

B: Praise him, all his angels,
       praise him, all you choirs of heaven.

C: Praise him, sun and moon,
       praise him, all you shining stars.

B: Praise him, you highest heavens,
       you galaxies beyond the skies.

C: Let them praise the name of the Lord,
       for he commanded and they were created.
       God set them in place for ever and ever,
       and ordered that they will never pass away.

A: Praise the Lord from the earth!

B: Praise the Lord, you whales and octopuses,
        and creatures from even the deepest depths.

C: Praise God, you lightning and hail, snow and clouds,
        you storm winds that do his bidding.

B: Praise God, you mountains and hills,
        you flowering apple trees and spreading oaks.

C: Praise God, you wild animals and all the cows in the field,
        you mini-beasts who crawl and you birds that fly.

B: Praise God, you young men and women,
        you older people and children.

C: Praise God, all you prime ministers and presidents,
        all you heads of state and company directors.

B: Praise the name of the Lord,
        for God's name alone is exalted!

A: God's splendour is above the earth and the heavens.
        God has raised up for his people one who will rule us, who will save us –
        the praise of all his saints, the people close to his heart.

        (*In a whisper*) And his name is Jesus.

Richard Sharples

YUM, YUM, RUB MY TUM

With thanks to Psalm 65

ALL: YUM, YUM, RUB MY TUM.
        THANK YOU, GOD, FOR FOOD TO EAT.

A: You care for the earth and water it;
        you fill it with riches, its streams with water;
        you prepare the earth to give grain to its people.

ALL: YUM, YUM, RUB MY TUM.
        THANK YOU, GOD, FOR FOOD TO EAT.

B: You soak the furrows and level the ridges;
        you soften the ground with rain
        and bless the land with growth.

ALL: YUM, YUM, RUB MY TUM.
        THANK YOU, GOD, FOR FOOD TO EAT.

A: You crown the year with riches,
        and all that you touch comes alive:
        the untilled pastures yield crops,
        the hills are wreathed in joy.

ALL: YUM, YUM, RUB MY TUM.
        THANK YOU, GOD, FOR FOOD TO EAT.

B: The meadows are clothed with sheep
        and the valleys adorned with grain,
        so that with shouts of delight
        everything breaks into song.

ALL: YUM, YUM, RUB MY TUM.
        THANK YOU, GOD, FOR FOOD TO EAT. AMEN

Richard Sharples

THROUGH THE EYES OF A CHILD

When did you last take a walk outdoors with a child? Did you explore a tiny patch of green, an anthill, pebbles on a beach, an old tree stump? To cultivate a heart for creation in our society we need only take the hand of a child. The reactions of children to wildlife they see are often surprising … noisy, rambunctious youngsters will suddenly fall silent and gaze in awe.

Picture these scenes:

A hush falls over a class of young children as a deer steps out of the forest and crosses the trail in front of them.

Eyes peer at the hole high up in a tree trunk. A small face with tiny ears and a black mask peers back – the raccoon seems as interested in the children as they are in him.

Silently standing as still as statues, with arms outstretched, the five-year-olds wait patiently for one of the tiny black-and-white chickadees to collect a sunflower seed from their open palms. When a tiny bird lands on a young boy's hand you witness an expression of awe on his face!

This is what it is to experience the wonder of nature through the eyes of a child: tiny insects are creatures of amazement; mushrooms and moss create miniature worlds. Children can truly reveal to us the awe and wonder of a heart for creation. Their natural affinity with living things and genuine compassion can inspire us to do all that we can to protect the legacy of the natural world we leave to our children.

Unfortunately, many children today lack these opportunities to explore natural habitats. How can we find ways to provide access to natural environments for all children and allow them the freedom to explore the world of nature?

Walk in the woods, stop by a stream, wander through a meadow, or lie on your back and gaze at the stars … go out together to experience the world through the eyes of a child.

Fiona van Wissen

HEARTBEAT OF CREATION

I love trees: they stand naked in winter, and burst with new life in spring. If you take a stethoscope on a spring walk and look for a young smooth-barked tree, you can hear what sounds like a heartbeat through the stethoscope: The sound of sap being 'pumped' against gravity, up the tree to the tips of the leaves. It sounds like our own heartbeat, and I often think of it as the heartbeat of creation.

We are connected to trees closer than you might think. I am no biologist, so it stunned me to discover, that if you take a single molecule of chlorophyll you have over a hundred atoms of carbon dioxide, nitrogen and hydrogen arranged in a complex and exact pattern around a single atom of magnesium. Now take a single molecule of haemoglobin and you have that exact same pattern of carbon dioxide, nitrogen and hydrogen around a single atom of iron. That is the only difference, that tiny atom of iron or magnesium. We can truly follow St Francis, calling trees, and all sap-filled plants, our brother or sister.

Chris Polhill

SOMETHING DIFFERENT

There was something different about her, this young German with her punk outfit and flowing hair who wandered into the church where I was minister one morning, clutching her boyfriend's hand. Him we had seen before. He was a local lad – sullen, withdrawn, known to the police, getting by. But she was different.

They hadn't much money. Or much of anything really. They had been housed by the Council. A tiny flat up two flights of stairs, with a balcony facing the fire station.

It wasn't her punk outfit in the Sunday congregation that made her different. Nor her smile in that fragile partnership. It was the balcony. Her balcony. All the upstairs flats had balconies. They were either empty or littered with junk and damp washing. But not here.

Here, nasturtiums trailed over the railings, tomatoes were starting to blush and canes were in place for the runner beans. Soon there would be lettuces. She was pricking out the seedlings when I called. Despite the concrete landscape, despite the two flights of stairs, here there was contact with the earth and its cycles. And gentle, patient nurture. And faith in the future.

Brian Woodcock

HELPING HORSES AND THE ENVIRONMENT

In the eco-congregation of Christ Church Methodist/St John Southworth RC Nelson Lancashire we have developed a novel community link with the local horse rescue farm run by HAPPA (Horses and Ponies Protection Association), in nearby Briercliffe on the edge of the Pennines.

We have organised eight monthly Sunday afternoon nature trail walks at the farm. Led by one of our experts, many people have attended the walks, which include all ages going over stepping stones in the local river. We have seen interesting wildlife, including the smallest British bird of prey, the merlin. One church member photographed the wildlife and made a slide show on DVD. This was shown at our annual Creation Festival to much acclaim.

We are also involved in tree and hedge planting at the farm, and in the planning of the woodland garden. We have learned to appreciate how slow the processes often are with charities, relying on voluntary giving and help. Also, liaising with local authorities can take a very long time – but was worth the trouble for the grant we received towards the trees. We are working with the full-time staff, learning from them what is best for the horses, and making hedges in the fields for windbreaks.

Through this link, people have gained insights into the importance of caring for the natural environment, and have become more sensitive to the beautiful details in creation, so that they notice creation more generally. Some have helped to improve the trail, some to plant trees, but best of all, the increased visitor activity has helped the charity to help more horses.

Barry Dickinson

A CONVERSATION

This drama is based on Job 1:1, 2:1–10, where God and Satan are in conversation.

God is sitting in a chair and Satan struts round him as if in charge …

God: Well, well … the wanderer returns. Where on earth have you been? More worryingly, what have you been up to?

Satan: Oh, you know … strutting around the planet here and there. Ducking and diving, bobbing and weaving. I must say, God, you truly have excelled yourself this time. What a wonderful creation. So many colours and textures and intricate details. I love what you've done with the fiords of Norway, and the mountain ranges – who would have thought you could have invented so many shades of purple. Wonderful.

God: Well, I'm quite pleased with it myself. But I doubt you've come to pay a compliment. What have you *really* come here for?

Satan: Oh God, you are too cynical. Though now that you mention it, I *do* have an idea I'd like to propose ... Truly, you have made a wildly wonderful world. But how good is it really? Come on, God ... I see a flaw in the whole thing. You have created something on a massive scale. It knits together in the most ingenious ways. But I do believe there is a crucial glitch.

God: Oh? And that would be ...?

Satan: Why, the human being, of course. It was all very worthy of you to so imaginatively create a being in your image. Personally, I feel there is a little pride in that which is really not worthy of you, a little arrogance even, which will be this creation's downfall.

God: Nonsense. Look at my man Job. What do you make of him now? Still spiritual, moral, good-living. Still giving me total respect. Still steering clear of evil. He passed the acid test and his integrity's intact, even though, for no good reason, you were hell-bent on destroying him.

Satan: Yeah, but he's not exactly stereotypical, is he? I reckon that if you hit any human being with something really nasty – something that hurts physically, emotionally, spiritually – they'll spend their last breath cursing you.

God: Never.

Satan: I beg to differ. Give me the human and I'll prove to you how arrogant you have been, for humans will not only destroy themselves, they'll destroy your creation. Indeed, a person will give up beauty before they ever give up power. I am sure it's so.

God: Nonsense.

Satan: And a person will give up on justice – before they give up the coffee they drink.

God: I don't believe it is so.

Satan: And a person will turn a blind eye to a changing climate before they choose a different lifestyle.

God: Do you really think humans are that shallow? What about the good they do? They are wonderfully made. When you look in their eyes you see a reflection of love. When you create each one's fingerprints, or whisper their name, calling them into the world, they are in the image of heaven. When you fill a flower with perfume, or colour an autumn leaf with sunsets, you know their souls soar with the breath and beauty of it.

Satan: Yes, but when a person does not get what they want, they will curse you to your face. They will take the good, but not the bad. Simple fair-weather fans. Worse still, they'll deny their part in the web of creation. They will believe they stand against it, willing to fight it, as ruler, as sovereign ...

God: You think so? Well, have your way with them then. Take the human and see if it is true. I created them with a love that is part of their every atom. They will know the truth, they will see the wonder, they will live in justice, they will share what I have given them, and they will step lightly in this world. They will not covet it, but care for it. It is how I created them. And they know their Creator.

Satan: We'll see, we'll see ...

God: Yes, we shall ...

Roddy Hamilton and Ruth Bell

IN THE BEGINNING: A CREATION DRAMA

Voice 1: In the beginning, before God created the heavens and the earth, there was nothing. And God said:

Voice 2: Y'he! *(cymbals crash)*. Let there be light ...

Voice 1: Through the Word all things came into being and the Spirit of God swept over the face of the void. In the first minute of time, the universe stretched a million billion miles across. Two minutes more and God had made 98 per-cent of all the matter there is or ever will be *(pause)* ... Perhaps about nine billion years passed *(pause)* ... And God caught up a swirl of gas and dust 24 billion kilometres wide and from almost all that gas and dust God made our sun. But around it still spun the dust grains that became its planets. God spent two million years fashioning planet Earth.

Children toss an inflatable globe back and forth across the central space.

Voice 3: And God saw that it was good. There was evening and there was morning, the first day ...

Voice 1: About 500 million years later, God said:

Voice 2: Let there be life.

Voice 1: And beneath sulphurous vapours in boiling seas bacteria swarmed. And some became blue-greens who could photosynthesise.

Two children walk on covered with blue and green crepe-paper strips, blowing bubbles.

Voice 1: The blue-greens sent up bubbles of oxygen – like beads of silver on the sur-face of the deep – and over millennia these transformed the atmosphere and built the ozone layer.

Voice 3: And God saw that it was good. There was evening and there was morning, the second day ...

Voice 1: And God said:

Voice 2: Let the waters bring forth swarms of living creatures.

Voice 1: Plants grew in the seas. Corals and sponges formed.

Children walk on wriggling crepe-paper worms on sticks.

Voice 1:   Worms and jellyfish swam, then trilobites and ammonites. God made fish about 160 million years after the ammonites.

Voice 3:   And there was evening and there was morning, the third day ...

Voice 1:   And God said:

Voice 2:   Let the earth put forth vegetation: plants yielding seed and trees of every kind.

Voice 1:   And it was so.

A child wheels in a barrow of plants and sets them down somewhere central (e.g. around the bottom of the altar).

Voice 1:   God planted mosses and liverworts along the shoreline. And sowed the horsetail and club mosses that would become coal. God planted the ferns that waved amongst them and the pine trees and the cedars that towered above.

Voice 3:   And God saw that it was good.

Voice 1:   And God said:

Voice 2:   Let the earth bring forth creeping things and insects that fly.

Voice 1:   And it was so.

Children walk on carrying insect mobiles.

Voice 1:   Millipedes crept through the mosses and silverfish slid across the ground. Amphibians – some of them four metres long! – dominated the earth for about 100 million years. Grasshoppers chirped and the blue dragonflies hovered overhead.

Voice 3:   And God saw that it was good. There was evening and there was morning, the fourth day ...

Voice 1:   And then God created the great land monsters that were the dinosaurs, and also the tortoise and the snake, and then the opossum.

Children walk on with model dinosaurs they hold up to show folk.

Voice 1:   And 180 million years ago, God said:

Voice 2:   Let the waters under the sky be split into smaller seas and dry land spread around the globe.

Voice 1:   And God split the plates of the Earth asunder, and the continent of Pangaea broke up and moved about the Earth.

Voice 3:   And God saw that it was good. There was evening and there was morning, the fifth day ...

Voice 1:   And God said:

Voice 2:   Let these lands be filled with wild animals of every kind, and let birds fly above the earth across the dome of the sky; let plants bring forth flowers and great fish swim the seas.

Voice 1:   And all this was so, for God created the wild animals of the earth and the birds of the air, the flowering plants and the giants of the deep. 65 million years ago the climate changed and the earth grew cold and the dinosaurs died. And then God made many more wondrous creatures. And perhaps just three million years ago, or perhaps less than a hundred thousand, God said:

Voice 2:   Let there be humankind, made in God's image, that they may delight in these works and create and share in the husbandry of the fish of the sea, and of the birds of the air, and of every living thing that moves upon the earth.

Two dads carry on large boxes marked as if posted, and lift their babies out.

Voice 1:   So God created humankind, male and female, in God's image.

Voice 3:   God looked at everything – and indeed it was very good. There was evening and there was morning, the sixth day ...

Voice 1:   And on the seventh day, God rested. *(Pause)* ...

But God's creating had not stopped nor were the plates of the Earth stilled. And in their scriptures people celebrated a God who watches over the calving of the deer and helps the lion hunt its prey, who fathered the rain and gave birth to the ice, who gave the horse its might and by whose wisdom the hawk soars.

And God so loved this world that he became flesh and dwelt among us.

This is the world of the Lord.

Joanna Laynesmith

WE CHOOSE GOD

We choose a world of justice.
WHERE GOD'S RESOURCES ARE CARED FOR AND SHARED FAIRLY.
WHERE WE CONSERVE CREATION FOR FUTURE GENERATIONS.
WHERE ALL PEOPLE CAN LIVE IN PEACE.

We choose,
WE CHOOSE GOD, FOR GOD IS JUSTICE.

We choose a world of peace.
WHERE GOD'S CHILDREN NO LONGER DESTROY EACH OTHER.
WHERE EVERYONE IS TREATED WITH RESPECT FOR THEIR UNIQUENESS.
WHERE LASTING PEACE IS BUILT ON GOD'S LOVE.

We choose,
WE CHOOSE GOD, FOR GOD IS PEACE.

We choose a world of love.
WHERE GOD'S LOVE IS KNOWN TO ALL THE CHILDREN OF THE EARTH.
WHERE EVERYONE CAN FEEL ACCEPTED BY THEIR BROTHERS AND SISTERS.
WHERE GOD'S PURPOSE FOR THE WORLD IS FINALLY REVEALED.

We choose,
WE CHOOSE GOD, FOR GOD IS LOVE.

We choose a world of joy.
WHERE THE JOY OF GOD IN ALL CREATION IS CELEBRATED.
WHERE THE GOODNESS WITHIN ALL IS GLADLY KNOWN.
WHERE WE JOIN CREATION'S SONG OF PRAISE.

We choose,
WE CHOOSE JOY, FOR GOD IS JOY.

We choose,
WE CHOOSE GOD.

AMEN

Michael Davidson

MAKER GOD

Maker God,
I am made in your image:
I am a maker too.

When I am writing
I feel your joy in me,
your imagination dances in me
telling me 'Yes'.

When I am digging
I feel your laughter in me,
I meet worms in the soil,
leaves brush my hands
birds sing.

When I am praying
I feel your hope in me,
sometimes your sadness too.
I am held
in your life.

You rejoice
in your creativity.

You made me
in your image.

I love being
a maker too.

Ruth Burgess

SILVER WHISPERS

Listen ...
the universe is singing.
Silver whispers from star to star,
the roar of the golden sun,
the blue Earth's dance in the darkness.

Listen ...
the great drum, the solemn sea
pulsing under the moon,
the heartbeat of the sleeping land,
the crackle and snap of air.

Listen ...
the living creatures are singing:
each little life lifts its voice,
sings, swells and stutters to a stop,
passes its song to children's children.

Listen ...
we who have ears to hear, and the gift of speech,
love the song, gather it up and sing it.
Bring words of worship and wonder,
sing for the sun and stars,
sing for the earth and all its creatures.
Tell out, shout – the beauty and the bounty of it!
Sing creation's song to the Creator!

Marnie Barrell

BIRCHES

The trees in Sutherland would make you weep.
Coming down Berriedale Braes in the spring,
and the birches swooping down in a wild arc
(like great bending birds would open a wing
and embrace you) enfold you in green,

dark and passionate to squeeze the breath from you
and leave your heart racing and your cheek pressed
to roughness of bark.
Oh I can smell the intoxicating resin
and the sap of spring in my veins.

Kathy Galloway

THE GARDEN LAWN

Blades of green grass, seed heads bursting,
dance and quiver in a sultry summer breeze –
a sprinkling of daisies and yellow-throated buttercups
surrounded by flies and midges and bees.

A few dead leaves and some painted pink petals
provide protective cover for red ants rummaging
in the jungled undergrowth crawling with food,
spending their insect days searching and foraging.

A ground beetle bumps into a red-spotted ladybird
and goes on its way ignoring and ignorant
passing an earwig and many-footed millipede
searching for manna in the age-old way.

A desiccating earthworm sadly took a wrong turn
and twists in the warmth of the life-denying sun.
A black-and-golden honeybee hovers there in front of me
before flying on again to make more honey for tea.

Who would have thought it? Who could conceive it?
A whole city in the lawn and I didn't even know it.
Surely there's something there for a would-be minor poet?

Bryan Owen

IN THE INNER CITY

Creation is praising her God
in the inner city.

Window boxes,
burst into life.
The city park opens its gates,
to welcome the day.
Secret roof gardens
give glory to highest heaven.

Forgotten waste ground,
decked with willow herb,
makes space for the urban fox to hide,
for birds to sing and be heard.

In the cracks,
where pavement meets factory wall,
poppies spring up,
flashing orange and red.

People occupy borrowed ground
with plants and shrubs,
with pathways and picnics,
till the Council is ready to build.

Between the cars,
against the odds,
a butterfly weaves its unsteady dance
to the Risen One.

Creation is praising her God!
Join her now in celebrating
all that tend seeds of life
in unexpected places.

Brian Woodcock

MORNING HYMN

I sat on the old wooden veranda
early one gentle morning.
Heavy rain had awoken me
but the night's sticky air had cleared
with the rising of the sun.

I sat watching the waves
crashing on the reef not far distant
as they had been doing
for millions of years
before men and women wondered why.

The dark, heavy rain clouds slowly thinned
and as the light of a new day strengthened
God used all the colours in the Divine palette
to paint the sky
in lighter shades of glory.

A fruit bat flew home to roost –
her night's work done.
A silver dew covered the grass
as the mynah bird sang her morning song.
I sat entranced
at the start of this perfect new day
and thanked God I was alive.

Bryan Owen

WONDER AT CREATION

God of sunset and tsunami,
of snowflake and avalanche,
revitalise within us the heart of the child
who watched a leaf drift in the wind,
and a stone fall into a still pond.
May we always wonder at the scale
and richness of your creation,
learning to live by the spirit of harmony

and interdependence
that lies at the heart of your natural order.

Grant this, our prayer,
in the name of Jesus,
who said that a single wildflower
is more glorious than Israel's greatest king.

John Polhill

PRAYERS FOR THE SEASONS

Advent/early winter

Creation waits in eager expectation
for your new dawn to break in upon us
and banish the darkness
of sin and death. Amen

Christmas/midwinter

Almighty God,
in the sorrowful darkness
of our wintry earth,
you shed upon us the new light
of your Incarnate Word. Amen

Epiphany/late winter

Almighty God,
by wisdom you laid the earth's foundations:
grant us wisdom to discern your grace
in the gift of your self in Christ
and in the awakening earth. Amen

Lent/early spring

Almighty God,
you hate nothing that you have made.
As the earth brings forth new life
create in us new and contrite hearts
that we may receive perfect forgiveness

through the blood of Jesus Christ. Amen

Easter/high spring

Lord of all life and power
renewing the whole of creation:
we offer ourselves as its first fruits,
since Christ conquered death once for all,
restoring our hope and kindling our joy. Amen

Pentecost/early summer

Holy Spirit, present to all our senses –
in bodily warmth and purging fire
in breath of our lungs and rushing wind
in refreshing drink and drowning river
in provided food and dust of death –
inspire us to speak in your tongue. Amen

Trinity/high summer

Creator, Redeemer, Sustainer,
you manifest your wisdom
in the variety and unity of nature.
Teach us to respond in joyful obedience.
Amen

Creationtide/autumn

Creator God,
with all our brothers and sisters
we bless you, who give us life
in all its fullness. Amen

Kingdom season/late autumn

Almighty God,
keep your church in unity and peace
under Christ our Lord and Head,
and bring the whole created order
to worship at his feet. Amen

Eleanor Harris

THE HOLY ENCIRCLING

The concept of loving encircling is written deep within universal life.

We can give glimpses of that as we image, in words and symbols, a God who embraces all that is, and the planet that nurtures and feeds us if we will, in turn, do the same for its life.

The following can be used as a final act within a worship service, or as the gathering up of thoughts after a discussion on creation.

Different people can be invited to read the sections of the prayer and children may like to place the symbols.

You will need:

A long gold cloth to represent the love of God
Baskets of flowers, leaves, branches, fruit
A bowl of water
Rocks and a bowl of earth
Felt 'footsteps' to image humankind
Three large candles

The embrace of God

Leader: The love of God encircles all that is
           and universal life is embraced with grace.
           The Christ expands the loaves and fishes
           and feeds the waiting people with hope.
           The Spirit breathes within golden winds of care
           and watches over the infinite mystery of creation.

           The long gold cloth is formed into a large circle.

Leader: Hold us, touch us each day
           with your healing, nurturing energy, O God.

ALL: INSPIRE US TO VALUE EVERY PART OF LIFE
           IN HONOUR OF YOUR DREAM FOR ALL ETERNITY.

The embrace of creation

Leader: Creator, Redeemer and Wise Spirit,
we thank you that creation itself
embraces us in nurturing life.
It lifts our hearts in beauty and grandeur.

The flowers are placed inside the circle, within God's embrace.

Leader: We give thanks for all that is, O God.

ALL: MAY WE NEVER TAKE ANY OF YOUR GIFTS FOR GRANTED,
FOR THEY ENCIRCLE OUR LIVES IN ENDLESS GIFTS OF HOPE.

Leader: Creation enhances our well-being every day,
encircling us with care.

The leaves, branches and fruit are placed inside the circle.

Leader: We give thanks for all that is, O God.

ALL: MAY WE GUARD THE LIFE WHICH GIVES SO MUCH TO US,
AND CHERISH ALL THAT LIVES, IN ACTS OF SHARING AND JUSTICE.

Leader: The water of life, so precious and so vulnerable,
flows among us and between us for the survival of all.

The bowl of water is placed inside the circle.

Leader: We give thanks for all that is, O God.

ALL: INSPIRE US TO VALUE EVERY DROP OF THIS GIFT
AND TO SO LIVE THAT ITS PRESENCE NEVER LEAVES US.

Leader: And below our feet are the rocks and strengths of the earth itself.

The rocks and bowl of earth are placed inside the circle.

Leader: We give thanks for all that is, O God.

ALL: WE THANK YOU FOR THE STRONG, DEEP RESOURCES
WHICH LIE BENEATH OUR FEET,

SO EARTHY THEY SEEM ORDINARY
AND YET SO CRUCIAL TO ALL THAT LIVES –
THE INFINITE SIGNS OF YOUR FIRM AND NEVER-ENDING LOVE FOR US,
O GOD.

Our embracing

Leader: We will embrace creation
in a small and vulnerable circle of care.

We now turn our feet towards its life in humble gratitude.

ALL: WE WILL, AT LAST, RECOGNISE THAT OUR ACTIONS
CAN DESTROY OR SUSTAIN GOD'S GIFTS.
WE WILL WALK REVERENTLY UPON THE EARTH ITSELF
AS THOUGH OUR EVERY FOOTSTEP IS A PRIVILEGE.

The felt 'footsteps' are placed facing the circle.

The light of God

Leader: The light of the Loving Parent is held high
over all things in hope and grace.

ALL: THE LIGHT OF CHRIST REVEALS THE WORD FOR OUR FUTURE,
AND THE WARM FLAME OF THE HOLY SPIRIT WILL LEAD US ON.

The three candles are placed in the centre of the circle and lit.

Leader: Let us walk on in peace.

ALL: IN THE NAME OF CHRIST.
AMEN

Dorothy McRae-McMahon, Uniting Church in Australia

I WILL LIGHT A LIGHT

All members of the congregation hold unlit candles. There is a central candle with symbols of nature/creation and environmental work placed around it. Leaders (A,B,C) take their light from this candle.

A: I will light a light
      in the name of the Maker of light,
      who lit the world with sun, moon and stars
      and breathed the breath of life
      into all things.

      A lights their candle.

B: I will light a light
      in the name of the Revealer of light,
      who brought light into the darkness
      and stretched out his hands for us,
      giving his love to the whole world.

      B lights their candle.

C: I will light a light
      in the name of the Inspirer of light,
      who lit the world from within
      and fills our lives with wonder
      in the search for learning and wisdom.

      C lights their candle.

      Then A, B and C share their light with the others around them. The light is passed on through the worship space until everyone's candle is lit.

A: We hold these lights:

ALL: FOR THE TRINITY OF LIGHT AND LOVE:
      GOD'S PRESENCE EVERYWHERE,
      GOD'S SALVATION FOR EVERYONE,
      GOD'S INSPIRATION IN ALL THINGS.

B: We hold these lights:

ALL: FOR OURSELVES AND EACH OTHER,
     FOR OUR FAMILIES, FRIENDS AND ENEMIES,
     FOR OUR WORK, HOPES AND STRUGGLES.

C: We hold these lights:

ALL: FOR THOSE IN NEED.
     FOR PEOPLE AND CHURCHES
     SUFFERING DISCRIMINATION AND PERSECUTION.
     FOR FUTURE PEACE AND JUSTICE IN COUNTRIES
     WHERE THERE IS WAR AND INJUSTICE.

A: We hold these lights to give thanks:

ALL: FOR WATER, AIR AND SOIL,
     FOR PLANTS, TREES AND ANIMALS,
     FOR ROCKS AND MINERALS,
     FOR SEASONS AND SUSTAINABILITY.

     MAY OUR FOOTPRINT ON THIS EARTH BE LIGHT.
     MAY WE DISCOVER YOUR HOLY PRESENCE EVERYWHERE.
     MAY WE VALUE YOUR GIFTS WITHOUT HARM OR WASTE.
     MAY WE INCREASE OUR SENSE OF BEAUTY IN EVERYTHING WE MAKE AND USE.

     AMEN

Robin Morrison

PRAYER FOR A HARVEST

Creator God,
we thank you for a harvest safely gathered in.
We ask for your blessing on those who work this land
and know the sea,
and who bear the stresses of bringing food
to our tables.

You stud this landscape with scarlet poppies,
tremble the air with birdsong,
and flash brilliance from dragonfly wings.

Help us to care deeply for all that you have made
and to protect its beauty and abundance.
Through your Son Jesus Christ,
who took delight in creation
as he walked, rested and spent time with you. Amen

Julia Morris

THANK YOU FOR ORDINARY WONDERFUL THINGS

Thank you, God, for the colour of tomatoes and beetroot,
for the different colours and shapes and fragrances of flowers,
for grubby potatoes and funny-shaped carrots –
for the goodness of the earth itself.

Thank you, God, for the taste of apples from the tree –
of blackberries picked straight from the hedgerow;
for the glossiness of conkers and acorns ...

Thank you, God, for the smell of baking cakes and real coffee.
For the smell of wood smoke and damp leaves;
and for the lights of home on a dark evening.

Thank you, God, for the kiss of a dog's wet nose and
for the purring contentedness of a cat.

For all of these ordinary wonderful things – thank you, God.
May we never forget to give thanks to you, Maker and Giver of all.
Amen

Richard Sharples

FOR US TODAY

The different objects are brought forward during a hymn. Following the hymn they are placed, one by one, on the communion table.

Tablecloth

Person 1:   Blue-flowered flax waved in a soft breeze.
Did it know it would become the tablecloth for our table
set for communion, today?

Plate of bread

Person 2:   Golden wheat lay ripening in the sun.
Did it know it would become our loaf
that breaks open heaven's meal, today?

Jug of water

Person 3:   Water in a sparkling burn gurgled through the moor.
Did it know it would become our water of baptism
for God's own people, today?

Goblet of wine

Person 4:   A clasp of ripening grapes dithered on the vine.
Did it know it would become our good wine
for this cup of grace, today?

Candle

Person 5:   A beehive buzzed and worked the flower rows.
Did it know its comb would become our symbol
of Christ's light, today?

Bible

Person 6:   A world turned in the depths of space.
Did it know its dawn would dance with the sacraments of
bread, water and wine for us today?

Roddy Hamilton

COME TO THE TABLE

Voice 1:   I remember the time of creation, of choosing colour and texture, mountain height and valley depth. I remember how God sculpted love into it all – every nook and cranny alive with the promise of heaven. And we give thanks for it all: its richest splendour and darkest secret.

Voice 2:   I remember the parting of the waters, the choice of Moses to follow God into the wilderness, the elements against them but the promise before them – choosing to go where God led: into a future where water flowed from rock and manna waited in the morning. And we give thanks for it all: the story of Exodus, of the Red Sea and the land of milk and honey.

Voice 3:   I remember the prophet Joel's voice calling the people of Israel to choose a new way of living: to care for the widow and the orphan and to know what would happen if they carried on as they were. And we give thanks for it all: the choice to hear God's longing for a new world, and to change and follow it.

Voice 4:   I remember John the Baptist, who lived in the wilds and spoke of a new heaven and earth, and shouted at the world to choose a new way of living that recognised justice; who took water and blessed its use. And we give thanks for it all: being newborn into a world renewed by our right living.

Voice 5:   I remember Jesus Christ, who upset the tables in the temple. And who later took bread and wine, the simplest of food, and blessed and broke it and shared it with people like ourselves. This bread and wine speaks of our choice to follow Jesus into a world renewed by love, where all creation rejoices in God.

Come and choose to eat and drink and belong to this new community:
a way of living that will not let go of the world:
a way of loving that is willing to make the difficult choices,
loving enough to stick by all that is broken and bring it to new birth.

Jesus said, 'Come, follow me. Come eat and drink, and know I go before you.'

Roddy Hamilton

BLESS US ON A GREY DAY

Living God, your creation blesses us in so many ways –
first light of dawn, sun's sparkle on a raindrop ...
we don't need to list them out for you.
There are days when they carry us, lift us over rocks,
and sweep us out of danger.

So bless us on a grey day, in a cold wet night,
in blistering heat, in storm, and when the sky is dark with dust.
We'll know because we'll hear 'I love you, child of my heart.'
We'll be standing so tall we will touch the sky
and we'll have a smile for everyone.

John Polhill

SHAKE US ALIVE

May there always be two thousand acres of sky above us.
May there always be the story of the earth beneath us.
May there always be the song of the air between us.
And may the love that shook creation from God's hand,
shake us alive,
that we may walk God's way,
now and always.

Roddy Hamilton

GOD'S LIGHT AND LOVE

As the air sings with songs of glory,
as the water flashes with the silver of creation,
as the forests bloom with leaves for the healing of nations,
so may God's light and love
fill our hearts and souls and minds.

From Eco-congregation

IN THE BEGINNING

In the beginning
love and darkness.
IN THE BEGINNING, GOD.

In the dancing
stardust and planets.
IN THE DANCING, GOD.

In the making
seas and mountains.
IN THE MAKING, GOD.

In the laughing
pterodactyls and crickets.
IN THE LAUGHING, GOD.

In the risking
Eve and Adam.
IN THE RISKING, GOD.

In the healing
Zacchaeus and Jesus.
IN THE HEALING, GOD.

In the journey
pain and justice.
IN THE JOURNEY, GOD.

In the ending
home and glory.
IN THE ENDING, GOD.

Ruth Burgess

OH THE LIFE OF THE WORLD

Words: Kathy Galloway; music: Ian Galloway; arrangement John L. Bell

Oh the life of the world is a joy and a treasure,
unfolding in beauty the green-growing tree,
the changing of seasons in mountain and valley
the stars and the bright restless sea.

Oh the life of the world is a fountain of goodness
overflowing in labour and passion and pain,
in the sound of the city and the silence of wisdom,
in the birth of a child once again.

Oh the life of the world is the source of our healing.
It rises in laughter and wells up in song;
it springs from the care of the poor and the broken
and refreshes where justice is strong.

So give thanks for the life and give love to the Maker
and rejoice in the gift of the bright risen Son.
And walk in the peace and the power of the Spirit
till the days of our living are done.

Kathy Galloway
Music: Ian Galloway; arrangement: John L. Bell

TOUCH THE EARTH LIGHTLY

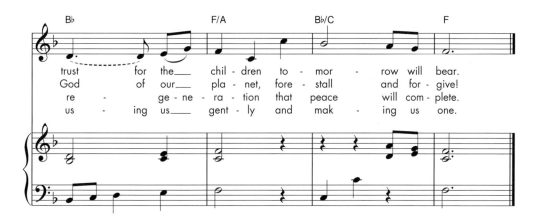

trust		for	the____	chil - dren	to -	mor	-	row will	bear.
God		of	our____	pla - net,	fore -	stall		and for -	give!
re	-		ge - ne - ra - tion	that	peace		will com -	plete.
us	-	ing	us____	gent - ly	and	mak	-	ing us	one.

Touch the earth lightly,
use the earth gently,
nourish the life of the world in our care:
gift of great wonder,
ours to surrender,
trust for the children tomorrow will bear.

We who endanger,
who create hunger,
agents of death for all creatures that live,
we who would foster
clouds of disaster,
God of our planet, forestall and forgive!

Let there be greening,
birth from the burning,
water that blesses and air that is sweet,
health in God's garden,
hope in God's children,
regeneration that peace will complete.

God of all living,
God of all loving,
God of the seedling, the snow and the sun,
teach us, deflect us,
Christ re-connect us,
using us gently and making us one.

Shirley Erena Murray

WHAT THE LORD CREATES

Tune: Twinkle, twinkle, little star

Praise him, praise him, praise the Lord
for the wonders of the world.
For the people big and small,
for the animals short and tall:
we will care for all these things
that our Lord Creator brings.

Praise him, praise him, praise the Lord
for the wonders of the world.
For the sea and for the sky,
for the animals and birds that fly:
we will care for all these things
that our Lord Creator brings.

Praise him, praise him, praise the Lord
for the wonders of the world.
For the seasons of the year,
for the plants that reappear:
we will care for all these things
that our Lord Creator brings.

Praise him, praise him, praise the Lord
for the wonders of the world.

Joanna, Emily and Sam Crawshaw

This hymn won first prize in the children's section of Christian Ecology Link's hymn competition.

LAMENTING THE DAMAGE
TO CREATION

LAMENTATION: THE PUBLIC VOICING OF PAIN

Deep peace of the running wave to you,
deep peace of the flowing air to you,
deep peace of the quiet earth to you,
deep peace of the shining stars to you,
deep peace of the Son of peace to you.

The Celts spoke of the 'little book' that was the Bible and the 'great book' that was creation – and they read God in both. This Gaelic blessing, often used on Iona, comes from a time when people could believe with all their hearts in the deep peace of the creation. Humankind might rage and contend across borders and continents, empires might rise and fall, men and women might flower and die, to be blown away like grass in the wind, but the running wave, the flowing air, the quiet earth, the shining stars, these things would endure unchanging, promising deep peace in their stability, their beauty and their purity. Even further back are these words versified from St Patrick's Breastplate, that great hymn of encompassing:

> *I bind unto myself today*
> *the virtues of the starlit heaven,*
> *the glorious sun's life-giving ray,*
> *the whiteness of the moon at even,*
> *the flashing of the lightning free,*
> *the whirling wind's tempestuous shocks,*
> *the stable earth, the deep salt sea*
> *around the old eternal rocks.*

Today, we know that the earth, which seemed to our ancestors to be unchanging, unassailable and enduring, is actually in endless transition, that change is its only constant. Of course, the changes take place on a timescale almost unimaginable to us, over millennia upon millennia, and mostly they are invisible to us, except where scientists have been able to interpret their observations. But we also know now that the pace of change – geological, climatic, ecological – has been vastly accelerated by human activity and the evidence of that is all around us, visible and indeed unavoidable.

'For I do not do the good I want, but the evil I do not want is what I do', wrote St Paul in another context. Humankind has not deliberately sought to degrade and destroy its habitat; mostly it has sought to improve it, for the human species at any rate. But the determination to bend the earth to the will of humankind, to see ourselves as creator not created and the failure to recognise ourselves as a species among species, inextricably interdependent, is a judgement now being read back to us.

To be creature, one among many, is to come face-to-face with our limitations. We are not God, and God is not just an idealised version of us. God is other, and speaks to us in other voices. Our judgement of the world, sometimes expressed as if we had a monopoly on divine truth, is in truth that which holds us most to account. In Micah 6, the prophet calls the people as if to a court of law to listen to what God is saying, and this is what God the plaintiff says:

> *Arise, plead your case before the mountains,*
> *and let the hills hear your voice.*
> *Hear, you mountains, the controversy of the Lord,*
> *and you enduring foundations of the earth;*
> *for the Lord has a controversy with his people,*
> *and he will contend with Israel.*

There can be no clearer indication anywhere in scripture that to be creature in the covenant is to be required to be in right relationship not only with our own humankind, but with the whole creation. Justice is also eco-justice. And how then, will the mountains judge us? Will the enduring foundations of the earth find in our favour? In the last thirty years alone, the human species has destroyed one-third of its non-renewable resources. Our actions have consequences: the destruction of rainforests leads to global warming; the pollution of lakes destroys localised ecosystems; the earth resists soil erosion and the loss of biodiversity with floodwater, but the floods drown and bring diseases in their wake. We are losing around 10,000 species of life every year. How will the mountains judge us? I think we are beginning to hear the answer.

This is loss that we can barely comprehend. It is a shaking of the foundations of life. The familiar landscape is changing – not just the physical but the intellectual and spiritual landscape – and we are losing our bearings. We are gradually being exiled from the certainties about the world expressed by the poetic Celtic words. The experience of exile is part of the Scottish collective memory. In the 19th century, many thousands of Scots were driven by hunger or cleared off the land into industrial cities, or even out of Scotland altogether, often to the other side of the world. They sang the same psalms and songs of exile as the people of Israel, as refugees and forced migrants have done in many times and places. In this poetry we can hear the lament and the longing for a beloved land, for the beauty of its glens and mountains and rivers, for its communal and cultural life. They remembered what they had loved and lost, and they lamented. Their hope was for return. There was always the assumption that the land itself would still be there, unchanging in its reality.

But that assumption is no longer true for the people of the Maldives, whose islands home is likely to be drowned as sea levels rise with global warming. Already they are exploring the possibility of a new home for a whole population. The trauma involved in such a relocation can only be imagined. Such drowning will affect islands and coastal cities across the globe. The Maldives are only one example of the vast geographic changes already underway, from the rainforests of the Amazon to the high Alps of Europe, from the Arctic melts to the agricultural lands of Australasia. I lament that my children, born and raised in lowland Scotland, have hardly known what it is like to go sledging in the snow, as I did only a generation ago. But my lament is only a faint echo of those far more vulnerable in other places.

People in pastoral ministry learn about the stages of grief: the shock, the denial, the anger, the deep sadness. In the West, perhaps we are somewhere between denial and anger. But the sadness will come, as it has for those who have either experienced or studied in depth the scale of what is happening. Such immense sorrow can have a paralysing effect. The biblical tradition of lamentation – the public voicing of pain – is one important way in which people in huge crisis have responded and sought to find a way through their disempowerment. The Book of Lamentations, sitting firmly in the middle of the prophetic books of the Hebrew Bible, laments the fall of Jerusalem and the beginning of the Babylonian captivity. Its poems are still used today in Jewish liturgy. It has allowed people to name their loss, their complicity and their fear, to turn passive despair into active mourning and to release the energy trapped in maintaining denial into energy for action and change. Lamentation has been an important aspect of all movements for justice, peace and freedom.

In a culture which is terrified of failure, loss and grief, finding the appropriate spaces for lamentation is not easy, but I think it is essential. A sense of place, a profound love of a particular landscape, is a deep human instinct, even when that landscape does not appeal to everyone. In his moving and beautiful book *Palestinian Walks*, Raja Shehadeh describes a territory that has often been found bleak, barren and intimidating to visitors – with the eyes of love and a different way of seeing. It is a remembering of a place that is already disappearing through environmental degradation. Many find the remote wilderness places of Scotland, the bare hills and strange rock formations, equally challenging. To me, they are beautiful beyond compare.

We need ways of remembering and naming, in sorrow and anger, what we have loved, even as it is under threat. To release these is also to release our power for repentance and change. Liturgy has always been a way of doing this, what Walter Brueggemann has called 'liturgical resistance'.

> *I'm going to miss the birds, singing all their songs.*
> *I'm going to miss the wind, been kissing me so long,*

sing Antony and the Johnsons, in a lament from popular culture. Time is running out fast. Now is time for anger and sorrow that liberates us for action.

Kathy Galloway

LAMENTING THE DAMAGE
TO CREATION:
LITURGICAL RESOURCES

OPEN OUR HEARTS

Before the God who loves us with great compassion
WE COME WITH OUR SORROWS.

For the damage to this planet,
WE ARE WEEPING, CREATOR GOD.

For the unequal consequences for the poor,
WE ARE WEEPING, SHEPHERDING GOD.

For the denials and fears within us,
WE ARE WEEPING, HOLY GOD.

Loving God, take away the fears that freeze us
and give us the courage to live out your compassionate justice.
AMEN

Creator God,
we offer to your love
all denial of climate change
and its consequences:
deaf to the cries of the poor;
blind to the troubling damage to creation.

Lead us into your truth.
Heal the fear that binds us.
Open our eyes to see,
our ears to hear
and our hearts to respond,
for your love's sake.
Amen

Chris Polhill

FORGIVE OUR GREED

Leader: We come before God, lamenting our lack of care and hardness of heart,
            that we might be forgiven:

ALL: FATHER, OPEN OUR EYES TO SEE:

A: Those who scratch at the earth
            only to find the dust of our disregard.

B: Those who plead for a fair share
            with tongues swollen by hunger.

A: Those who beg for justice
            with hands scarred by torture.

B: Those who cast nets into seas
            emptied by commercial profit.

ALL: FATHER, FORGIVE OUR GREED.

Leader: God of the harvest,
            harrow our hard hearts;
            lay bare our selfishness;
            help us see that our unwillingness
            to share the earth's resources fairly
            is costing lives every minute of the day.

ALL: FATHER, FORGIVE US AND CHANGE US. AMEN

Julia Morris

PRAYER OF CONFESSION AND FORGIVENESS

In our actions and our failure to act, we confess our sins:

LOVING GOD,
WE CONFESS THAT WE HAVE REGARDED LUXURIES AS NEEDS.

WE CONFESS THAT WE HAVE TOO MUCH
WHILE OTHERS DO NOT HAVE ENOUGH.

WE CONFESS THAT OUR MONEY IS OFTEN INVESTED IN COMPANIES
WHO DEAL UNETHICALLY AND UNFAIRLY.
WE CONFESS THAT WE OFTEN SPEND OUR MONEY
WITH LITTLE THOUGHT ABOUT THE IMPACT OF OUR SPENDING ON OTHERS.

WE CONFESS THAT OUR LIFESTYLES ARE CAUSING CHANGES IN THE GLOBAL CLIMATE.
CHANGES WHICH POOR PEOPLE ARE THE FIRST TO SUFFER FROM.

Loving God, convict us by your Spirit,
and then forgive us, that we may live to show mercy,
do justice, and walk humbly with you, our God.
In Jesus' name, we ask it.

AMEN

Richard Sharples

GOD OF CREATION AND CARE

God of creation and care,
YOU DREAMT OF A WORLD OF BEAUTY AND BALANCE ...
BUT WE HAVE NOT REALISED YOUR DREAM.

You separated night from day,
establishing a world of patterns and rhythms:
WE CONFESS THAT WE HAVE IGNORED AND INTERRUPTED THOSE CYCLES –
REMAKING THE WORLD AS CHAOS AND CONFUSION.

You separated sky, water and land,
establishing a world of habitats and homesteads:

WE CONFESS THAT WE HAVE DESTROYED AND DISRUPTED THAT BELONGING –
REMAKING THE WORLD WITH DISPLACEMENT AND DISLOCATION.

You gave fertility to air, sea and earth,
establishing a world of plenteous sufficiency for all:
WE CONFESS THAT WE HAVE PLUNDERED AND POLLUTED THAT TREASURE STORE –
REMAKING THE WORLD BARE AND BARREN.

You looked at the world
and saw that it was good.
WE LOOK AT IT AND SEE
THAT IT IS SO MUCH LESS
THAN YOU DREAMT IT TO BE.
FORGIVE US.

Pat Bennett

RAINBOW PRAYER FOR OPERATION NOAH

Creator God, how deep are your designs!
You made a living earth, cloud, rain and wind,
and charged us with their care.
We confess that the way we live today
is changing the climate,
the seas and the balance of life,
dispossessing the poor and future generations.
Build our lives into an ark for all creation,
and, as you promised Noah never to repeat the Flood,
so make us heralds of a new rainbow covenant:
choosing life for all that is at risk –
for creation,
for neighbours near and far,
our children and ourselves.

From the Operation Noah launch, Coventry Cathedral, 2004

Operation Noah is informed by the science of climate change, motivated by our faith to care for creation and driven by the hope that our society can be transformed and enriched through radical change in lifestyles and patterns of consumption.
(From the Operation Noah website www.operationnoah.org)

SEEKING A NEW RELATIONSHIP

Creating God, you give light and life,
and express delight in your creation.
You gave the command to till and care for your garden,
but we have abused the beauty of creation and the keeping of your work.

WE CONFESS THE PLUNDERING OF FINITE RESOURCES.
WE CONFESS TO STEALING OUR DESCENDANTS' BIRTHRIGHT TO LIFE.
WE CONFESS THE FLAGRANT POLLUTION OF LAND, SEA AND AIR.
WE CONFESS THE CHURCHES' LACK OF CONCERN
FOR THE WELL-BEING OF CREATION.
WE CONFESS THE EXCESSES WITHIN OUR OWN LIFESTYLE.
CREATING GOD, WE HAVE DESECRATED YOUR CREATION
AND DARKENED YOUR LIGHT.

In a moment of quiet, we confess our profligate lifestyle and human greed ...

Words of renewal

God of life and light,
as we seek a new relationship with your created order,
may we sense the grace and peace
of a new relationship with you.
AMEN

From Eco-congregation

CARBON CREATURES' CONFESSION

A: God, your love made it possible for the first particles of matter
      to dance with energy,
      linking each other in space and time.

B: Carbon creatures came into being and learnt to walk tall,
      placing their feet firmly on the ground of your garden,
      breathing the mystery of your breath,
      enjoying your inspiration and reaching up to the skies.

A: As you look at us now, your carbon creatures,
      what can you see through our carbon emissions?
      Do they scratch your eyes and mar your looking?

B: Out of your energy of love
      came heat and light for our warmth and growth.

ALL: OUT OF OUR ENERGY PRODUCTION AND USE
      COMES BOTH HELP AND HARM.

A: Out of your energy
      came sacrifice and self-giving.

ALL: OUT OF OUR ENERGY USE
      COMES GREED AND SELF-INTEREST.

B: Out of your energy
      came creativity, freedom and inspiration.

ALL: OUT OF OUR ENERGY
      COMES COMPROMISE,
      COMPLACENCY AND VIOLENCE.

      GOD, TEACH US TO LOOK WITH YOUR SEEING;
      TO HEAR WITH YOUR HEARING;
      TO COMMIT WITH YOUR WILLING;
      TO FEEL WITH YOUR FEELING;
      TO CARE WITH YOUR HEART:
      TO LIVE IN YOUR LOVE.

      AMEN

Robin Morrison

A GRIEVING FOR CREATION

You need dried leaves, a bowl and water for this confession. Different people can be the Leader for different sections.

Leader: The earth heaves in alarm
            and the oceans rise in protest as each year passes.
            The tears of the planet have dried up in desolation,
            and the colours of creation are paled into despair.

ALL: WE, WHO LIVE AND WATCH ALONGSIDE THE PAIN AND LONGING,
            GRIEVE OUR PRESENT AND OUR PAST.

            Dried leaves are placed on the communion table.

Leader: O God, we have often used and dominated your creation
            as though it owes us everything.
            Many of us have consumed more than we need,
            without the gratitude of cherishing in return.

            Silent reflection

Leader: Our hearts cry out in remorse for our neglect,
            in the face of the gracious gifts from you
            which have surrounded us over the ages.

ALL: MAY THE TEARS OF OUR SHAME
            BE TRANSFORMED INTO THE NURTURING
            FOR WHICH CREATION HAS LONG WAITED.

            Water is poured into a bowl beside the leaves.

Leader: May our grieving go far beyond
            the horizons of our words, O God.

ALL: MAY WE BE PART OF THE BEGINNING
            OF A NEW DAWNING OF HOPE
            FOR ALL THAT LIVES AND GROWS AND HAS ITS BEING.

            The leaves are placed in the water.

Leader: Hear our prayers, Creator God.
            Be known in the way we live,
            in the respecting of all which surrounds us
            and in our commitment to the restoring of life.

ALL: AMEN.

            Assurance of pardon

Leader: God, who is the source of all life and all good,
            listens to our grieving with love.
            We are never left without mercy
            as God goes on creating newness in us and all things.
            We are forgiven.

ALL: THANKS BE TO GOD.

Dorothy McRae-McMahon, Uniting Church in Australia

A VERSION OF PSALM 10

A: Why are you so far away, O God?
        So elusive when we have greatest need of you?

B: Look how wicked people are oppressing the weak
        by consuming scarce resources and causing disasters.

A: They flaunt their wealth to become famous,
        having no regard for your Gospel.
        They mock those who put their faith in you
        and claim that life has no purpose.

B: They put their trust in wealth and power
        and believe that they are in control.

A: Their lifestyle is one of self-seeking pleasure;
        they have no regard for the damage they do.

B: They play on the weakness of others
        to ensnare them in their own folly.

A: They accept no responsibility for the state of the world,
        looking only for ways to protect themselves.

B: They think that their desires are paramount
        and see no need to justify their actions.

A: We long to see them brought down,
       for the oppressed to take power.
       Why should these people be free to act selfishly
       and think they will never face the consequences?

B: We believe that you share the misery and pain
       of all the oppressed and exploited,
       that you stand beside the weak
       and are torn as creation suffers.

A: We want to end the power of evil
       and bring about your kingdom here.
       Today, give us strength to name wrongful acts
       and to listen to the cries of the poor.

B: Show us how to bring about fairer societies
       where everyone has a chance.
       So that no one goes in fear for themselves,
       their loved ones, or the places they treasure.

John Polhill

CURE OF A BANNED CELEBRITY

There was a conference on waste reduction at which Jesus was invited to be the keynote speaker. Now, it happened that a minor celebrity had had a rather good idea about how to reduce the amount of industrial waste, and she was keen to present her idea to the conference.

However, because the celebrity was known to have lived in a very wasteful way, the conference organisers would not allow her to speak because they feared it would bring bad publicity. The celebrity's friends, on the other hand, were very supportive of her idea, so they sneaked her into the conference and got her onto the stage near where Jesus was sitting.

When Jesus saw the celebrity he said, 'My friend, you can be forgiven for what you have done wrong in the past.' The leaders of the conference became very annoyed, thinking to themselves: *What right does Jesus have to say that all the waste this woman has created counts for nothing?* But Jesus, who realised what they were thinking, said, 'Is it easier to free this woman from her guilt, or to accept her plans for waste reduction? But to prove to you that we should not judge people by their past behaviour': And he turned to the woman and said: ' ... Go outside and explain your plans to the media and your ideas will become the highlight of the conference.'

    All the people attending the conference were amazed and said: 'My goodness, we have seen strange things today!'

John Polhill

PARABLE OF THE SOWER

A farmer went out to sow
and sowed a field of maize,
and as the farmer scattered the seed
it bounced as it landed on the earth.
Some fell on the pathways where the soil was packed hard
from the long walk of refugees,
whose lands were now dry and infertile;
or owned by agribusiness for mono-cropping.

Some fell on rocky ground where there was little soil.
Ancient forests had been removed for ranch farming;
and while the corn grew for a year or so, soon the soil was exhausted,
and the land became a desert washed of all its nutrients,
and no crops could grow.

Some fell among thorn bushes that choked the plants,
because no one was there to farm the land.
Conflict or subsidy had left this land empty,
letting those in poorer countries export their crops to where the lands were fallow,
while the poor could grow little for themselves.

But some seed fell in good soil,
and the plants produced corn,
some a thousand grains, others five hundred, others one hundred.
Then this was used to produce ethanol for cars,
and high-quality feed for cattle and chickens.

And the world sowed the seed
but was listening to the wrong kind of profit.

Roddy Hamilton

THE EARTH SPEAKS

In the beginning,
I saw you, oh blessed Gardener.
The trees in my fields did clap their hands,
and I shouted with joy –
for here was the one whom our Creator had appointed,
ordained to shape my growth
with light touch and simple delight.

Yet, in your waywardness,
driven by your internal lack,
you have looked on me with lustful eyes and
your delight has turned to insatiable consumption.
Your dominion has turned sour
and I now groan under your heavy hand.

In the beginning,
I opened myself to receive you,
to bear you, my Gardener, the fruit of our tender union.
In return you have plundered me to my core.
You have vomited your sordid chemicals
into my womb and
your pollutions have poisoned my fertility.
My rivers have now nowhere they can go
to clean themselves;
they have become arteries of death,
perverting the growth of all that drink from them.

Why, oh Gardener, have you forced yourself upon me?
Why have you trampled upon my face and
bent my back with the burden of your demands and requirements?

I lie now bare before you, as I always have;
your ordained dominion remains.
Choose to end your tyranny over me,
restore your muddied image
and join with me once more
in tending to the creation as our Maker wishes.

Phil Smith

KEEPING FOOD UNDER WRAPS

I remember hearing a fridge defined as 'a place where you store your food before throwing it away'. Recent research suggests this is no joke.

The Waste and Resources Action Programme (WRAP) has produced research suggesting that people in the UK needlessly throw away 6.7 million tonnes of food each year. Now, no one I know has enough money, desperate times and all that. But, apparently, everyone has got enough food to throw away – untouched – about a fifth of their stockpile.

A mum on the radio explained the problem: 'The trouble is, you go into the supermarket to buy some milk, but the milk is always put at the far end; so you get all this other stuff in your face first – and the cakes look so good you have to put one or two in the basket.' This is true. How often I heard the following, when I worked in a supermarket. As I packed the customer's fifth bag they would say: 'And I only came in for some milk!' My record was serving a customer who 'only came in for some milk', and spent £73.

We are clearly buying too much, as the UK statistics show. And how about this? Every household in the UK throws away about 18% of its food; and those with children, 27%. And what are we throwing away in particular? Well, 5500 whole chickens get the old heave-ho every day, followed closely by 440,000 ready meals – again, daily. (No, I can hardly believe it either.)

Bread and potatoes were the two foods most commonly thrown away when they could very well be eaten. And spare a thought for the tragic yoghurt. Yoghurt is the single most abandoned item, with 1.3 million unopened cartons going the way of the bin every 24 hours. So, that is more than 2 million pointlessly killed chickens a year, and more than 60 million yoghurts joining everything else on our ballooning landfill sites.

The Environment Minister said that the findings were 'staggering'. He added: 'There are climate costs to all of us in growing, processing, packaging, transporting and refrigerating the food we throw away.'

We need the prophets of old to induce some much-needed shelf-reflection. Let Jeremiah weep for the prematurely exiled ready meals. Let Hosea long for the restoration of the perfectly edible potatoes. Amos shall denounce the basket of summer fruit casually thrown away; and Malachi proclaim the great day of the yoghurt. Let Ezekiel envision the new supermarket, where milk is not always at the far end. And by the landfill site, choking with methane gas, let us hear again the writer of Lamentations: 'Is it nothing to you, you who pass by?'

Until the new food dawn, even our most famous of prayers may need an extra line: 'Give us today our daily bread – that we might throw most of it away.'

Simon Parke

THE PRODIGAL CIVILISATION

This is better memorised and told, and is best done relatively deadpan. One person crosses repeatedly from one side of the 'stage' to the other to indicate the different parallel stories, or two people stand side by side taking their parts alternately.

There was a man who had two sons.

There was a God who, over thousands and millions of years, made a great creation, with a whole host of creatures upon an earth. And there came a time when one of those creatures came to understand themselves to be special in the eyes of God.

And the younger of them said to his father, 'Father, give me my share of the inheritance that is due to me.' And he divided his living between them.

And the humans said to God, 'Give us our inheritance,' and they plundered the earth with mines and drills and rigs, sucking out the black treasure, consuming it in their machines and spewing the gas into the sky.

Not many days later the younger son gathered all that he had and went on a journey to a far country, and there he squandered his inheritance in loose living.

A great economic system arose fuelled by deep-level passions, based on conspicuous consumption and using the black treasure. The people travelled everywhere and nowhere. Forests were destroyed. It was party time. The air was filled with laughter … But the clouds were gathering.

And when it had all gone, a great famine arose in the land and he began to be in want. So he went and joined himself to one of the citizens of that country, who sent him into his fields to feed the pigs. And he would gladly have eaten from the pigs' trough, but no one gave him anything.

It was the climate, you see. They hadn't thought of that. And once they had, it was too late. The animals and plants began just to disappear. The desert spread. The wells grew deeper. Water … Anxious people … Angry people … Violent people. The rich built castles. The poor made battering rams.

And then he realised; he said, 'Why even my father's hired servants have bread enough to spare but I perish here with hunger. I will arise and go to my father and say, "Father I have done wrong against heaven and against you. I am no longer worthy to be called your son; treat me as one of your hired servants."'

And a few began to dream of a home: they saw a vision of God surrounded by the creatures of the earth; they dreamt of living at peace with God and creation and they set out to make that vision real.

And he arose and set out for his father. And when he was far off his father saw him and had compassion and ran and embraced him.

And I will leave you to fill in the rest of the story.

Chris Sunderland

From EarthAbbey
www.earthabbey.com

TRINITY OF CREATION

Three people read this: a 'Creator', who is sculpting modelling-clay; a 'Sustainer', who is writing with a feather quill; and a 'Renewer', who is repairing some material with a needle and thread.

Creator: I have sculpted mountain ranges,
   and I gasp in wonder at the beauty
   that this act of love always reveals.
   I am the Creator.

Sustainer: In the past you were told 'an eye for an eye'.
   No longer: now 'love your enemy'.
   Only this is sustainable living.
   I am the Sustainer.

Renewer: Who believes creation is finished,
   completed and done for all time?
   There is yet more hidden beauty.
   I am the Renewer.

Creator: I have loved creation
   out of primordial chaos
   into the dance of the cosmos.
   I have balanced it all
   and let it loose to live.

When human greed distorts life,
the loss twists all out of sync.
When conceit unbalances life,
snowcaps slide,
deserts groan,
forests struggle.

I bear the pain.
I am the Creator.

Sustainer: Take only your need for today,
live in balance,
live in love with the world.

Hatred of enemy is not sustainable;
storing up treasures is not sustainable;
ignoring your neighbour's need is not sustainable.
This is not my way.

I am the way.
I am the Sustainer.

Renewer: I am the world's life force.
I bring buds to flower,
persuade grass to grow,
ice caps to shrink and renew.

Imbalance threatens hope,
hopelessness threatens the future.
Live today in a way that blesses the future.

Work with me to renew life,
I am the Renewer.

Creator: Live in love with creation.

Sustainer: Live in balance with all life.

Renewer: Live to renew the world.

Creator, Sustainer, Renewer: We are the three-in-one, your God.
O people of the world,
listen and hear.

Roddy Hamilton

AFFIRMATION

With the whole church
WE AFFIRM
THAT WE ARE MADE IN GOD'S IMAGE,
BEFRIENDED BY CHRIST, EMPOWERED BY THE SPIRIT.

With people everywhere
WE AFFIRM
GOD'S GOODNESS AT THE HEART OF HUMANITY,
PLANTED MORE DEEPLY THAN ALL THAT IS WRONG.

With all creation
WE CELEBRATE
THE MIRACLE AND WONDER OF LIFE,
THE UNFOLDING PURPOSES OF GOD,
FOREVER AT WORK IN OURSELVES AND THE WORLD.

Iona Abbey Worship Book

APORIA

How shall we live in the years that are coming
how shall we love and live in the loving
when so many fears on tenuous threads
hang over our lives and over our heads?

How shall we sing the songs of our living
how shall we hear the music of being
when in the bright sky even the lark
fears the gathering storm and approaching dark?

How shall we know the bluebirds are winging
how shall we know the good earth is breathing
when oceans are warm and winds blow too strong
when we know that our living has badly gone wrong?

So how will we live in the years that are coming
how can we love and live in the loving
when so many fears on tenuous threads
still hang over our lives and over our heads?

Bryan Owen

LAKE CHAD, AND OTHER DISASTERS

Once a lake was here,
green-growing surrounded;
many mammals watered;
village living sustained.
Dried out by climate change,
we lament its passing.

Once the river flowed here,
now another nation dams it;
their wish for water, our lack,
their greed? their need? our loss.
Sharing lost to climate change,
we lament the failure.

Once the fields grew green here,
now the water drowns them;
river spills a barrier;
muddied homes are stinking.
Flooded out by climate change,
we lament the losses.

Creator God,
we lament the damage
caused by climate change.
Inform our ignorance;
forgive our greed;
and grant us the wisdom
to make amends.

Chris Polhill

THE RED LIST

Creation's song
laments the passing
of Holdridge's Toad;
Baiji; Tasmanian Wolf.
Sings a mourning song
for Black Mamo;
Passenger Pigeon; Carolina Parakeet.
Grieves the loss
of *Undulata Delissea*;
Galipea Ossana; Hawaii Chaff Flower.

Grieves the loss,
endless the names
that sob through song.
From tiny insect to great mammal,
creation's celebrities
wounded to death.

Then beseeching, pleading,
the music crescendos

protect the threatened Black Lion Tamarin;
the Fishing Cat; Iberian Lynx.
Shelter the endangered Blue-throated Macaw;
the Mallee Emu-wren; the Araripe Manakin.
Conserve the disappearing Moon Trefoil;
the Jellyfish Tree; *Rafflesia Magnifica.*

Care for the earth
and the skies above;
restore the harmony
of creation's song.

Chris Polhill

www.iucnredlist.org

WE ARE THE PASSERS-BY

We are the new Romans,
imperialistic, materialistic, pragmatic,
stamping our 'one size fits all'
monoculture across the globe,
leaving our mark from pole to pole.

We are the new Pharisees,
blinkered, defensive of our realm,
full of spin, anxious of our place in the pecking order,
holding on to the advantages
of a lifestyle made in our own image,
willing to sacrifice the life of the voiceless
for our comfort and gain.

We are the passers-by,
seeing the suffering of the Christ of creation
on the cross –
Christ through whom the whole cosmos has its being –
and we walk on by,
unwilling to step out from amongst the crowd,
to stand up for life and be changed.

Simon Davis

THE HALF LAND

I travel in the half
world
between day and night
winter and spring,
long light
and its fading.

I look and see
the land become
the sea
become
the island
become
castle,
the ruin,
harbour,
a smudge of sand,
become
again

the sea.

I lie between
waking
and sleeping,
living
and dying,
in marram grass
clinging to hope in
the half
land,

now here

now gone.

And in my dreams
you come,
walking over
waves
turning
the fish in
the pan to sate
my hunger,
swelling and breaking
foaming and forming.

Then fading again,
like the mist
over the shore
between the last scatter of
the world's end houses
huddling like lost sheep
into the hollow
of the last
of the land.

And in my dreams
you come.

And in my dreams

you go.

Alison Swinfen

FROM THE DARK SIDE

A burn of sparkling water gurgled through the moor.
Did it know it was becoming contaminated
with polycyclic aromatic hydrocarbons,
pesticides, potentially toxic elements
all along the way?

A field of wheat lay ripening in the sun.
Did it know it would never become a loaf,
because violent storms,
fuelled by changing global climate,
would flatten it before harvest time?

A clasp of ripening grapes dithered on a vine.
Did it know it would become good wine,
but never tasted,
because unfair trade practices
would prevent its sale in developed countries?

A hardwood tree stretched and shaded an ancient forest.
Did it know it would soon be cut down
to make way for an unsustainable
biodiesel production zone?

A beehive buzzed and worked the flower rows.
Did the bees know their days were numbered;
their population already in decline
because of human interference
in global biogeochemical cycles?

A world turns in the depths of space.
Do its people know how little time they really have?

Christine Davidson

THE THREAT TO THE PLANET

In the article 'The Threat to the Planet' in the *New York Review of Books* in July 2006, Jim Hansen, Director of the NASA Goddard Institute for Space Studies and Adjunct Professor of Earth and Environmental Studies at Columbia University, expresses his personal views about climate change.

Hansen states that we have two choices: continuing as usual; or altering our habits to keep climate change to a 2°F/1°C increase. Already plants and animals are migrating north, or higher up mountains to be at the temperatures they need for survival, and there is considerable risk of the interdependency between species being broken, and leading to more loss of animals and plants. Hansen suggests that if we continue as usual the temperature increase will be about 5°F/3°C. In this scenario the changes will happen too quickly for species to adapt, but more serious will be the changes caused by the ice melting in the sea. Ice sheets have changed according to the Earth's temperature throughout history, and that history gives us accurate information about sea levels in the past. When the Earth was last 5°F/3°C warmer, the sea was about 24m/80ft higher; at 2°F/1°C warmer, the sea was 4.8m/16ft higher. Of course, this sea rise does not happen all at once; in a hundred years it would rise about 6m/20ft, and about 0.9m/3ft respectively.

So continuing as usual and not altering our habits would cause global chaos affecting food sources and the places many humans live. Changing so that the temperature increase is lower would not only give plants and animals more time to adapt, but allow humans to contain and adapt to the new sea levels.

Hansen makes a number of suggestions for action, among them a carbon tax. He challenges the commercial interests that keep denial of climate change disproportionately presented in the media, and challenges governments, particularly his own in the USA, to co-operate and make the necessary changes, as we did when CFCs threatened the ozone layer. He regards the present time as a tipping point for the changes needed, as the longer we delay, the harder it will be to keep the temperature rise sufficiently low.

The article is very clearly expressed and accessible. To read it yourself go to: www.nybooks.com/articles/19131

Prayer

Living God,
from ice melting to polar bears dying,
we are damaging your creation.
Forgive us and free us from fear and denial.
May your Spirit so envision us,
that governments gladly choose
policies for healing and gentle change.
Bless us, so that our lives honour your gift of life.

Chris Polhill

SAVE THE POLAR BEAR

That image of a polar bear,
huge feet on tiny ice floe,
unable to walk the distance,
find the food it always did,
that image haunts me.

It speaks of ice melting,
seas rising,
hunger and restriction,
the possibility of ending,
another species gone.

Land going under rising sea,
that touches humans too.
Could New York, Mumbai, Venice,
fertile food-growing farms, also
slip beneath the waves?

'Save the polar bear,' we cry,
and we should mean it.
For, God help us,
save the polar bear
will save the humans too.

Chris Polhill

MORE ...

Lord, help us.
For these days we know so much more!

We know more about the mechanics of the world
but think less about its well-being.

We know more about how its systems fit together
but care less about safeguarding those connections.

We know more about its cycles of life and death
but do less to follow their patterns.

We know more about the monetary value of its resources
but understand less about their true worth.

We know more about its other peoples
but are less tolerant of any differences.

Lord, help us!
For these days we know so much more,
but we have become so much less ...

Pat Bennett

LIFT US FROM DESPAIR

Lord, too often
we are blind
to the miracles of creation,
and deaf
to the cries of injustice.

Open our eyes, Lord,
to see the beauty of your world.
Open our ears
to hear the cry of the earth.
Open our hearts
to care for all living things.

Lift us from despair to hope,
from apathy to action,
from indifference to compassion.
Lift us and heal us,
for your love's sake.

Fiona van Wissen

BLESS OUR LAMENT

Creator God,
bless the tear we shed
    for the resources that we have squandered.
Bless the sigh we breathe out
    for the spoilt air and atmosphere.
Bless the head we hang
    for the creatures lost and exploited.
Bless the hands we wring
    for the things we have broken and wasted.
Bless us as we lament.
Cradle us as we regret.
Restore us as we start afresh.

John Polhill

TURN US, GOD

As the Earth turns
night to day
day to night
TURN US, GOD.

From our selfishness
night to day
day to night
TURN US, GOD.

From our foolishness
night to day
day to night
TURN US, GOD.

Towards justice
night to day
day to night
TURN US, GOD.

Towards loving
night to day
day to night
TURN US, GOD.

As the Earth turns
night to day
day to night
TURN US, GOD.

Ruth Burgess

GOD OUR MAKER, HEAR OUR CRY

Tune: Aus der tiefe (Heinlein)/Forty days and forty nights

God our Maker, hear our cry,
sorrow for our lack of care.
We have used your gifts for life
without thought and without prayer.

Gifts unfairly shared around,
though you gave enough for all.
We preferred to store up wealth;
fear and greed has us in thrall.

We regret our carbon use
now we know it hurts the earth;
caught in systems hard to change,
lead us on a wiser path.

Breathe forgiveness over us,
free our souls to pay the price,
serve creation day by day,
follow Christ in sacrifice.

Chris Polhill

NOW IS THE TIME FOR A RECKONING

1 Now is the time for a reck - on - ing,
2 Si - lent the voi - ces in bush and tree,
3 We are the root of the earth's un - ease,
4 We are the spen - ders of pre - cious store,
5 We take the boun - ty of all you give,

now all is flower - ing and flou - rish - ing, God, help your chil - dren
si - lent the crea - tures of air and sea, God, help your chil - dren
we are the pi - rates who dredge the seas, God, help your chil - dren
we are the greed - y who take no score, God, help your chil - dren
we are the sor - row that makes you grieve, God, help your chil - dren

mind - ful - ly lis - ten: soon there may be just a si - lent spring.
mind - ful - ly lis - ten: ours are the hands that took earth for free.
mind - ful - ly lis - ten: ours is the creed do - ing as we please.
mind - ful - ly lis - ten: ours are the mouths want - ing more and more.
mind - ful - ly lis - ten: mind - ful - ly choose how the world will live!

Now is the time for a reckoning,
now all is flowering and flourishing,
   God, help your children
   mindfully listen:
soon there may be just a silent spring.

Silent the voices in bush and tree,
silent the creatures of air and sea,
   God, help your children
   mindfully listen:
ours are the hands that took earth for free.

We are the root of the earth's unease,
we are the pirates who dredge the seas,
   God, help your children
   mindfully listen:
ours is the creed doing as we please.

We are the spenders of precious store,
we are the greedy who take no score,
   God, help your children
   mindfully listen:
ours are the mouths wanting more and more.

We take the bounty of all you give,
we are the sorrow that makes you grieve,
   God, help your children
   mindfully listen:
mindfully choose how the world will live!

Shirley Erena Murray

ACTION FOR CHANGE

WHAT IS A DISCIPLE?

What is a disciple? A follower, a student, a trainee, a seeker? Something of all of these suggestions, but at the heart of it a disciple is someone who is growing to love in the same way as their Master loves. For a Christian this means growing to love the things that Jesus Christ loves and growing in a way of life that shows such love. Having a heart for creation means having the same heart commitment for people and creation that Jesus Christ has.

Jesus was not an ecologist in the modern sense, but his teaching makes it clear that he was a son of the soil, someone who had taken the time to contemplate the world around him and to learn from it. The area of Galilee where he grew up was a rich, lush, market garden area, full of farms and small holdings, topped by grazing areas in the hills, fringed with wilderness and big open skies. This world around him, bursting with God's provision and beauty, was as much his scripture as the scrolls of the synagogue he knew so well. For present-day followers, contemplating the natural world around us is a good start for being a disciple in God's world.

Through parables based on his observations of natural life around him, Jesus taught that God who cares for the birds of the air and takes delight in the transient flowers at the edge of the field cares for and takes delight in each of us, his children. He taught through the miracle of germination and growth that if our faithfulness was simple and honest it would grow like a mustard seed to become a great bush providing shelter and food for God's creatures. In the well-known parable of the sower, where a farmer sows seed so generously it falls on the path amidst the pebbles and the weeds as well as on good soil, Jesus reveals a God who is generous and gives all our souls, no matter how unpromising, the chance to bear a good harvest.

Contemplating the world around us today also reveals that the natural world is in crisis. The threat that humanity poses to the workings of our planet's ecology is very grave. Climate change and the pressure to acquire natural resources are already putting pressure on the world's poorest people, who often live on marginal land. As well as learning spiritual lessons from nature we need to reconnect with our human vocation as God's earth-keepers.

For the disciple justice is about action, pressing for and doing what is right for all that God loves. In the present ecological crisis Christ's love directs us to work for justice by maximising the God-given diversity of life on earth for the benefit of all the world's people and creatures, not just for the people in the wealthy developed areas of the world.

We have been hindered in this vocation for too long by a spirituality that has concentrated on human beings' individual relationship with God, forgetting the importance of community and that God has provided for all the world's people. At one time we did not understand the effect humanity has on our planet's ecology, but now we do, and must reform our spirituality, our convictions and our actions in the light of what we know.

Part of the problem is that often we confuse ourselves when thinking about 'the world', not sure if we mean the wonderful thing beneath our feet, or those ways of living, the unredeemed aspects of human culture, that St Paul warns us are against the flow of God's grace.

So on one hand, we are positive about creation, admiring it and drawing inspiration from the power, glory and beauty of God's work, which the creation stories in Genesis remind us is good. On the other hand, we are negative, looking towards our deliverance from the world into the bliss of the new heaven and the new earth promised in the Revelation of St John. Many hymns and writings are full of such mixed messages too, missing out what God is doing in the middle, within creation, between Genesis and Revelation!

That middle is just where we are now. So as disciples in God's troubled world we need to think again about what it means to be part of God's creation and what God wants us to do at this time.

Amazing as it is, we find the middle is just where God reveals what he is doing. Binding the fate of creation and the Son of God together by Jesus' birth in Bethlehem, God who gives life to all creation reveals an openness to the experience of creation: to joy in life, to suffering and death. The one who scatters the stars across the sky looks up at them with eyes like ours. The one who creates the natural processes of life, kind and cruel as they seem, experiences them as one of us.

Through the Cross and Resurrection the stitches that mend the tear in the fabric of creation are cast, bringing all things back to God in healing and wholeness. To be a disciple of Jesus is to be aware of being part of God's creation and Jesus' work of healing it, reconciling us to God, to each other and to the whole of the cosmos.

To have a heart for creation means living in the light of the knowledge that God loves each one of us, but that God's love is not limited to human beings. God loves the flowers, the sparrows … all creation. The New Testament writers bore witness to this, believing that Jesus died not just to reconcile people to God, but to reconcile all things, every-thing in creation.

For our discipleship, growing in loving what Jesus loves means doing what is just: loving creation as well as our human neighbours, taking special care to lift the poor and marginalised, who are the first to suffer in times of crisis. It means loving those who are our neighbours in time and space. And making choices for the good of creation so that generations to come can still enjoy creation as a home that is growing and developing in the freedom God has given it.

Such a conviction leads us to look afresh at the scriptures and the world around, to contemplate and learn, to be humble in heart and willing to challenge many of the preconceptions we have grown up with, which come from a time when the planet seemed to have endless capacity to absorb humanity's insatiable greed. It means daring to question and be different.

If we have a growing sense of having a heart for creation it will affect all we are and all we do. So beware! Love, as the song goes, changes everything. As a disciple of Jesus Christ, through whom all things in creation are made, it will change the way you travel around, the food on your plate and even the clothes on your back.

Despite the doom and gloom of the headlines with their warnings of a global ecological catastrophe, God has not finished his work with us yet and neither has he finished with his work in creation. We live in defining times for what it means to be human beings, growing from a collective adolescence in the way we treat our planet into a new maturity, as we find our place in partnership with God in caring for creation.

In Jesus Christ we have hope for the future, guided by the knowledge that when the work is done, we who are part of creation will share in its glory through the love of Jesus Christ, the Word of God, who sustains all creation and who has captivated our souls.

Simon Davis

A SIX-WEEK CHALLENGE

This is a six-week challenge to care more for God's 'big book', creation. Each day you will be presented with a fact, a challenge relevant to the fact, and a Bible passage, prayer or poem for reflection. You can take the six-week challenge at any time of the year. If you choose to follow it during Lent, there are extra resources included for Holy Week.

There is also a section for groups, designed to help folk support each other and reflect together on their experience of taking the challenge.

Each week explores a particular environmental theme. To prepare, read through the week you are about to do, and see if for any of the challenges you will need to collect, buy or research something. You may need to talk over some of the issues with others in your group or household beforehand.

Some of the facts or challenges might make you feel uncomfortable; dismissive; guilty; angry; disturbed … if so, remember the following:

- All of the above feelings show you have an active conscience.
- In the past we did not know that human activity was damaging the planet.
- We *should* feel disturbed by some of the changes to our planet.
- Lent is a good time to explore with God our difficult feelings.
- Healing is part of God's design.

While many of the facts are taken from UK sources, the six-week challenge is easily adaptable for use in other countries.

The facts and challenges for weeks 3, 4 and 5 were written and gathered by Katherine Shepherd of Marches Energy Agency www.mea.org.uk. The remainder of the six-week challenge was written and gathered by Chris and John Polhill.

Six weeks

'It usually takes about six weeks for something new to become part of your daily routine,' said the physio, as she taught me some new exercises for my back.

Six weeks
of remembering and doing
until something is part of you
and you do it instinctively every day.

Six weeks of walking
Six weeks of litter-picking
Six weeks of writing letters

Six weeks of growing vegetables
Six weeks of baking bread.

'It usually takes about six weeks for something new to become part of your daily routine.'

Do we need to wait for Lent?

Ruth Burgess

WEEK 1: WASTE

DAY 1

Fact: Freecycle is a web-based recycling service for all those who want to have something of theirs reused rather than thrown away. Everything posted or picked up must be free. www.freecycle.org

Challenge: Check your recycling and waste bins. Are you and those in your household recycling paper, card, glass, all cans, allowed plastic, tetra-paks?

Bible reading/prayer:

Remade

Living God, remake us,
collect the rubbish
scattered on the roadside,
hidden in the thicket;
all the careless discards
of our lives.

Refine them in the crucible
of your forgiving love.
Remould the greed,
Reweave the angers;
from all our wretched sin
your beauty bring.

Chris Polhill

DAY 2

Fact: In 2009, a leading supermarket gave away over 15 million 'Bags for Life', and recycled over 150 million plastic bags at their in-store facilities.

Challenge: Take a reusable shopping bag for all your shopping, and reuse any plastic bags you do take home.

Bible reading/prayer:

Time for remembering

Loving Lord Jesus,
you know how busy we are,
how much there is to do.

I thought your kingdom would be carefree,
and yet it seems to be burdened with care
... more things to remember, to be concerned about.

When you were busy, surrounded by crowds,
with their needs and their pleading,
you always had time for one more individual,
just because at the heart of your kingdom,
there was infinite compassion.

John Polhill

DAY 3

Fact: Some packaging is made from 'substandard' potatoes and can be composted.

Challenge: Check the layers of packaging that your shopping has. Aim for a maximum of two layers on items.

Bible reading/prayer:

Shopping in the Spirit

Living God,
thank you for the quiet campaigners
who vote with their shopping trolleys,

who choose what they buy,
who read the labels, count the wrappers
and speak to Customer Services.

Thank you for their commitment,
their undiminished vision,
their belief in the power to change.

Bless us when we swell their ranks,
when the power of the consumer
is the power of your Spirit.

John Polhill

DAY 4

Fact: Litter on UK beaches increased by 90% between 1994 and 2005. (Source: *BBC Wildlife*, Vol 124, no. 9, p.56)

Challenge: Litter-pick in a local public area – contact your local council to borrow safe equipment.

Bible reading/prayer:

He went to a country far away, where he wasted his money in reckless living. He spent everything he had. Then a severe famine spread over that country and he was left without a thing ... 'Father, I have sinned against God and against you. I am no longer fit to be called your son.' (Luke 15:13ff, Good News Bible)

DAY 5

Fact: Around 600 million batteries, which contain toxic ingredients, are sent to landfill every year. (Source: Environmental Data Information Exchange, www.edie.net)

Challenge: Check through the batteries that you use in appliances. Make a list, and as they wear out change as many as you can to rechargeable batteries. www.greenbatteries.com

Bible reading/Prayer:

Those who trust in the Lord for help will find their strength renewed. They will rise on wings like eagles; they will run and not get weary; they will walk and not grow weak. (Isaiah 40:31, Good News Bible)

DAY 6

Fact: The manufacturing of recycled paper uses 60% less water and 40% less energy than the manufacture of new paper. (Source: *ENDS Report 364*, May 2005, p.36)

Challenge: What goods do you buy that are made with recycled paper?

Bible reading/prayer:

The trees in the woods will shout for joy when the Lord comes to rule the earth. (Psalm 96:12, Good News Bible)

DAY 7

Fact: Over 75% of under-12s receive more than 10 toys a year, yet research shows that 67% of toys are discarded the year they are purchased. Many are just thrown away while still in working order. (Source: www.envirowise.gov.uk)

Challenge: Investigate whether there are toy libraries in your area. Have you toys you could donate? If there is a toy library, encourage others to use it.

Bible reading/prayer:

Play with us, Lord Jesus

Play with us, Lord Jesus,
a game that comforts all
the lonely empty places
deep within our spirit.

Play with us, Lord Jesus:
free us from 'must have now'
and 'want what they've got'
to just enjoy the moment.

Play with us, Lord Jesus:
set free imagination
to dream, and make, and explore –
to visit the moon in a cardboard box.

Chris Polhill

WEEK 2: CONSUMER CHOICE

DAY 1

Fact: The World Health Organisation reports 'the public concerns about GM [genetically modified] food and GMOs in general have had a significant impact on the marketing of GM products in the European Union'. Consumers have greater power than they realise.

Challenge: Organise your week so that you have at least two days when you don't buy anything at all.

Bible reading/prayer:

So God blessed the seventh day and hallowed it, because on it God rested from all work that he had done in creation. (NRSV)

DAY 2

Fact: Eating seasonal foods automatically leads to a greater variety in your diet. Other advantages of seasonal eating are promoted by charities like the Climate Group (www.eatseasonably.co.uk) and sites like www.eattheseasons.co.uk

Challenge: Research vegetable box schemes in your area by visiting
www.vegbox-recipes.co.uk
or by contacting the sustainability officer at your local council.

Bible reading/prayer:

Praise God for veg boxes

Fresh-cut spinach,
knobby celeriac,
spuds and toms and carrots –
thank God for veg boxes,
food, fresh and local.

Reconnect us to
the seasons,
to expectant waiting for
each flavour
in due time.

Forgive our demand
for perfect produce
wasting crops and labour.

Forgive the thoughtless greed,
the impatient demand,
ignoring costs
to earth and poorly paid.

God bless the eating
that honours all creation.

Chris Polhill

DAY 3

Fact: Advertisers believe they have the power to persuade you to buy their products. The total spending on advertising globally each year is many billions! In 2008, the total spending on advertising in the UK was £18.6 billion. (Source: The Advertising Association)

Challenge: Take a TV or magazine advert and *subvertise* it – e.g. cosmetic advert: 'Because your worth is our profit'; a new car advert: 'The drive for gridlock'.

Bible reading/prayer:

The wisdom to discern

Living God,
grant us the wisdom to discern
the real from the fantasy;
the need from the desire;
and truth from falsehood.
Give us your grace,
that we may seek only
the treasures of your kin-dom. Amen

Chris Polhill

DAY 4

Fact: Buying fair trade guarantees workers' rights and a fair price to producers.

Challenge: Look through your kitchen and clothes cupboards to see what fair trade goods you have. Resolve to increase this, and explore fair trade catalogues. Check the fair trade range in your local shops.

Bible reading/prayer:

Let justice roll down like waters, and righteousness like an everflowing stream. (NRSV)

DAY 5

Fact: Global spending on international tourism reached $946 billion in 2008. (Source: World Tourism Organisation). 'All-inclusive resorts' means that the money spent does not really benefit the local population.

Challenge: Plan a holiday that complies with eco-tourism standards – ask your travel agent about this or visit www.responsibletravel.com

Bible reading/prayer:

Soul-deep rest

In my need to rest,
help me, loving God,
to find gentle ways
to be refreshed.

To lie in your robe
surrounded by love;
know the warming breath
of your Spirit,
renewing, restoring.

Soul-deep the rest you give,
soul-deep your recreation.

Chris Polhill

DAY 6

Fact: Local churches near Carlisle changed stock in local supermarkets by informing them that they were only going to buy local (i.e. UK) or fair trade goods.

Challenge: Use only UK or fair trade ingredients in your meals today.

Bible reading/prayer:

Love the Lord your God with all your heart, with all your soul, with all your strength, and with all your mind; and love your neighbour as you love yourself. (Luke 10:27, Good News Bible)

DAY 7

Fact: Chemicals from cleaning products have been found in human tissue and breast milk; they also affect the land and sea through waste water. Some bacteria are good for you.

Challenge: List the all chemicals in the cleaning products in your home. See what you can find out about them. The Internet is helpful here.

Bible reading/prayer:

We are connected

We are sorry, Lord,
that just by living without thought
we pollute the air,
poison the waters
and damage the land.
We are sorry, Lord.

For we are connected,
whether we recognise it or not,
to all of creation;
to all that you made;
from ant to mountain
we are connected.

Holy Spirit,
heal and restore us,
that we may live gently on earth,
and all creation praise you,
the Living God,
Father, Son and Holy Spirit.

Chris Polhill

WEEK 3: ENERGY

DAY 1

Fact: If everyone in the UK always did the challenge below, we would together save enough energy in one year to power nearly every streetlight! (Source: Calor Gas Ltd)

Challenge: Next time you make a cup of tea, make sure you boil only the amount of water you need.

Bible reading/prayer:

Then God commanded, 'Let lights appear in the sky to separate day from night and to show the time when days, years, and religious festivals begin; they will shine in the sky to give light to the earth' – and it was done. So God made the two larger lights, the sun to rule over the day, and the moon to rule over the night; he also made the stars. (Genesis 1:14-16, Good News Bible)

DAY 2

Fact: Changing one incandescent ('normal') light bulb to an energy-saving light bulb could save you £2.50 a year, on average, and around £6 a year when replacing brighter bulbs or those used for more hours a day. (Source: UK Energy Saving Trust)

Challenge: During the next week, replace an incandescent light bulb with a low-energy bulb. If you have already changed all your bulbs to low-energy, encourage a friend or neighbour to do this.

Bible reading/prayer:

Touching

The dew glistens on the morning grass,
the air holds its breath for the first breeze,
the sun lingers shyly among the trees.

Are they waiting for me to splash my dark prints on the lawn,
to bestir the air with my eager passage,
to call forth the sun to light up my day?

It is my dream to sparkle with the dew and leave no sign of my passage,

to soar with the rising air and lie in its stillness,
to smile with the sun over some tiny joke we've learnt to share.

Is the world mine because I am in it,
or am I alien, scarring perfection by my very presence?

Is it my role to complete creation
or creation's role to complete me?

John Polhill

DAY 3

Fact: The average household could save £10-£80 a year by switching appliances off rather than leaving them on standby. The average saving is estimated to be £25. (Source: Energy Systems Research Unit, Strathclyde University)

Challenge: Go round your house and check that your TVs, DVD players, etc are switched off and not operating on standby.

Bible reading/prayer:

The bystander

You'll know where to find me:
I'll be on the edge of the crowd,
in the wings of the stage,
sitting by the phone,
looking out of the window.

I'm looking out for people who need help,
waiting to bring on the next scene
... to respond
... notice.

I don't want to get in people's way,
to upset them
to be a nuisance.

Just recently, I've imagined hearing a voice
... calling my name

... tugging at my controls
... pressing my buttons
... calling me out of the shadows.

'My dear one, don't be afraid, you're wanted on stage!'

John Polhill

DAY 4

Fact: For each minute a fridge door is open, it takes three energy-guzzling minutes for it to cool down again after you close the door. (Source: WWF South Africa) (Also: Bradford University; Ebico Ltd)

Challenge: Each time you open the fridge or freezer door this week, make sure you don't leave it open for any longer than is necessary.

Bible reading/prayer:

Be obedient to God, and do not allow your lives to be shaped by those desires you had when you were still ignorant. (1 Peter 1:14, Good News Bible)

DAY 5

Fact: Turning down your thermostat by just 1°C will reduce your heating bill by 10%. The recommended living room temperature is 21°C, and 18°C for the rest of the house.

Challenge: Try turning your thermostat down by 1°C, and if you do notice the difference, why not put on an extra layer or wear slippers? Feet are very important regulators of body temperature!

Bible reading/prayer:

The resting space

Lord, I fear the cold,
the chill of winter
that hurts my nose
with each breath;
freezes my toes;

shrivels my spirit,
so I long for
summer's warmth.
Want my home, the shops,
warm as summer.

Teach me nature's rhythm
for wintertime.
The resting space,
pause for thought;
the warmer clothes
and slanting light.
A gentle use
of earth's resources.

Chris Polhill

DAY 6

Fact: We use 800 million pounds worth of electricity on washing machines, tumble dryers and dishwashers in the UK. (Source: Climate Care)

Challenge: Today, avoid using these appliances. If you have wet clothes, hang them outside, if this is possible; and wash and dry your dishes by hand.

Bible reading/prayer:

Psalm 51

Generous in love – God, give grace!
Huge in mercy – wipe out my bad record.
Scrub away my guilt,
soak out my sins in your laundry.
I know how bad I have been;
my sins are staring me down.

You're the One I violated, and you've seen
it all, seen the full extent of my evil.
You have all the facts before you;
whatever you decide about me is fair.
I've been out of step with you for a long time,

in the wrong since before I was born.
What you're after is truth from the inside out.
Enter me, then; conceive a new, true life.

Soak me in your laundry and I'll come out clean,
scrub me and I'll have a snow-white life.

from The Message

DAY 7

Fact: The average household spends a third more on energy during the winter months than an energy-efficient home. (Source: Actionenergy, Energy & Technology Support Unit). Insulating your loft will reduce your heating bills by up to 20%; having cavity wall insulation, by 30%.

Challenge: During the next week, investigate how much insulation is in your loft. If your house has cavity walls, you may already know whether or not they are insulated. Call your local energy advice centre to find out about grants and installers in your area.

Bible reading/prayer:

Living flame of love
(After St John of the Cross)

Living flame of love,
so touch our hearts with your bright fire,
that we of tepid, even chilly faith,
may be alight with your passion,
and warm the globe with your love,
reflecting your care
for all of your creation. Amen

Chris Polhill

WEEK 4: TRANSPORT

DAY 1

Fact: About half of all car trips are for less than 5 miles. (Source: Factsheet on short car trips, Roger Mackett, Centre for Transport Studies, University College London, 2000)

Challenge: Write down the distances and purposes of all your car journeys during the next week and tick those for which you could have car-shared, used public transport, cycled or walked. Aim to use these alternatives in the future.

Bible reading/prayer:

Shared journeys

God who made us,
teach us to share –
the space on the train,
the chat on the bus –
and make friends of strangers.

God beside us,
teach us to share
the joy of the car,
to share the load,
never travel alone.

God All-Holy,
teach me to share
my life with you.
To let go control
of the driving wheel
into your Wisdom.

Chris Polhill

DAY 2

Fact: In 2006, air travel accounted for 6.4% of the UK's emissions of carbon dioxide, the main greenhouse gas causing climate change. Forecasts suggest that air traffic will grow. If no action is taken, carbon dioxide emissions from aviation could make up around 10% of the UK's total carbon dioxide emissions by 2020. (Source: Directgov website, www.direct.gov.uk, energy section)

Challenge: If you are planning to travel abroad this year, make time this week to investigate carbon offsetting schemes on the Internet or by contacting the sustainability officer at your local council. Research travelling to your destination by train or boat, or consider a UK holiday as an alternative.

Bible reading/prayer:

Traveller's psalm

As the train travels the track
and the ship sails the sea,
so my heart would travel with you –
my soul seeks the living God.

In the wonder of your works,
the beauty of God's creation:
high mountain and sunlit woodland,
the eternal movement of the sea,
and the rainbow spray of a long waterfall;
there I am refreshed by you,
my soul restored by your wonders.

Will the journeys have to cease?
Planet-saving carbon-cuts keep us local?

Will the hot sunny shores be empty of travellers?
Far-flung mountains with only local climbers?

Will I see distant family only on computer screen,
my heart longing for their touch?

Or will we find new gentle ways,
old trusty ways to travel?

All I know is that my journey with you never ends;

endlessly the soul travels with the living God.

So I will praise you each day –
sing of your glory wherever I am.

Chris Polhill

DAY 3

Fact: Flat tyres cost money and the environment: fuel consumption rises 2.5% for every 10 pounds per square inch a tyre is under-inflated. That's around £30 a year wasted by the average car! (Source: Tyre Industry Council/TyreSafe)

Challenge: During the next week, take time to check that the tyres on your car are inflated to the recommended level.

Bible reading/prayer:

A voice cries out, 'Prepare in the wilderness a road for the Lord! Clear the way in the desert for our God!' (Isaiah 40:3, Good News Bible)

DAY 4

Fact: In the UK, almost 6 out of 10 journeys taken to work are by car (57%). (Source: National Travel Survey, 2007, p.39). The long queues of cars during rush hour with only one occupant in each car confirm that there is great potential for car-sharing or using alternative modes of transportation.

Challenge: If you are travelling to the same destination as a friend or neighbour this week, arrange to car-share instead of using individual cars. Consider forming a car-sharing group at church.

Bible/prayer:

All the believers continued together in close fellowship and shared their belongings with one another. They would sell their property and possessions, and distribute the money among all, according to what each one needed. Day after day they met in the Temple, and they had meals together in their homes, eating with glad and humble hearts, praising God, and enjoying the goodwill of all the people. (Acts 2:44–47, Good News Bible)

DAY 5

Fact: In the UK around 43% of children are taken to school by car (Source: Office of National Statistics, 2008 statistic). Walking or car-sharing would help reduce the school-run impact. 'Walking buses' of children are another sociable and safe way to travel – collecting children along the route.

Challenge: Find out if there is a 'walking bus' scheme at your local school. If there isn't, suggest they start one.

Bible reading/prayer:

Protect our children

God our Creator,
protect our children
from idle car travel
and cotton wool living.

May they enjoy
walking's freedom,
seeing the little things,
and fresh-air living.

In the wonder
of your creating
may they notice you,
also beside them.

Chris Polhill

DAY 6

Fact: Traffic delays cost the UK around £20 billion a year (Source: *The Economic Costs of Road Congestion*, P. Goodwin, 2004). It is not always quicker to travel by car. Save time, money and stress by walking or using public transport, or plan your journey to avoid congested routes.

Challenge: Make a list of the journeys you *need* to make today. Consider how and when you travel so that you avoid congestion.

Bible reading/prayer:

Then Jesus sent them out to preach the Kingdom of God and to heal the sick, after saying to them, 'Take nothing with you for the journey: no stick, no beggar's bag, no food, no money, not even an extra shirt. Wherever you are welcomed, stay in the same house until you leave that town.' (Luke 9:2–4, Good News Bible)

DAY 7

Fact: Slow down – driving at high speeds significantly increases fuel consumption. Driving at 70 mph uses up to 15% more fuel than driving at 50 mph (Source: AA Fuel-saving tips) and increases polluting emissions by a similar percentage.

Challenge: Next time you are driving your car, reduce your speed to 50 mph. If you are a passenger, explain the above fact to the driver.

Bible reading/prayer:

A still centre

Be still,
and listen to the day,
touch the breeze
with the quiet in your soul.

Let the turning turbulence
of the hurly-burly rushing
and the busy dizzy people,
who never waste a second,
pass you by.

God bless you
with the quiet whisper,
which in all the day's doing
keeps a calm silent centre
in your being.

Chris Polhill

WEEK 5: WATER

DAY 1

Fact: Fixing a dripping tap can save as much as 5000 litres of water a year – if everyone in the UK fixed their dripping taps we would save enough water to supply 120,000 people in the UK with water for one day. (Source: Waterwise)

Challenge: Check the taps in your house. If there is a drip, arrange for a plumber to repair it.

Bible reading/prayer:

Jesus said to her, 'Everyone who drinks of this water will be thirsty again, but those who drink of the water that I will give them will never be thirsty. The water that I will give will become a spring of water gushing up to eternal life.' (John 4:13–14, NRSV)

DAY 2

Fact: If everyone in the UK who currently leaves the tap running when they brush their teeth turned it off instead, we would save 446 million litres of water a year – enough to supply 2.9 million people in the UK with water for one day. (Source: Waterwise)

Challenge: Next time you brush your teeth, remember to turn off the tap while brushing, or rinse from a tumbler.

Bible reading/prayer:

Forgive us

For the reservoirs that drowned people's homes,
forgive us, Lord.
For wasting water without thought,
forgive us, Lord.
For the many who still have only dirty water to drink,
forgive us, Lord.
For forgetting that water is a gift,
forgive us, Lord.
Bless those who will have to carry water to their home;
today, and every day, may we treasure each drop. Amen

Chris Polhill

DAY 3

Fact: Taking showers instead of baths will save enough water in a week for 1000 cups of tea! (Source: 'Green House', *National Geographic*)

Challenge: Take a shower instead of a bath today – for a maximum of two minutes.

Bible reading/prayer:

Showered with radiance

Lady Wisdom,
shower us with
your radiance;
enlightening, reflective.

Pour your waters
over our souls;
cleansing, reviving.

Baptise our dreams;
make them holy.

Wash away soul dirt,
as I cherish
your gift of water.

Chris Polhill

DAY 4

Fact: 30% of an average family's water use is flushed down the toilet.
(Source: Waterwise)

Challenge: Do not flush the toilet today unless you need to. If you do need to flush, use water collected from washing (bath, washing machine) or from running the tap to temperature, e.g. while waiting for hot water.

Bible reading/prayer:

They made camp at Rephidim, but there was no water to drink. They complained to Moses and said, 'Give us water to drink.'

Moses answered, 'Why are you complaining? Why are you putting the Lord to the test?'

But the people were very thirsty and continued to complain to Moses. They said, 'Why did you bring us out of Egypt? To kill us and our children and our livestock with thirst?'

Moses prayed earnestly to the Lord and said, 'What can I do with these people? They are almost ready to stone me.'

The Lord said to Moses, 'Take some of the leaders of Israel with you, and go on ahead of the people. Take along the stick with which you struck the Nile. I will stand before you on a rock at Mount Sinai. Strike the rock, and water will come out of it for the people to drink.'

Moses did so in the presence of the leaders of Israel.

The place was named Massah and Meribah, because the Israelites complained and put the Lord to the test when they asked, 'Is the Lord with us or not?' (Exodus 17:1b–7, Good News Bible)

Prayer

For our demands for water while others thirst,
forgive us and heal us, Holy God.

DAY 5

Fact: A garden sprinkler uses 1,000 litres of water an hour – that's nearly one pint every 2 seconds it is in operation. In a half an hour, it uses as much water as a family of four in a day. Lawns never need watering. (Source: Waterwise)

Challenge: Visit your garden centre and look at water systems that target specific plants, e.g. the soaker hose system; or encourage a friend or neighbour to be more water conscious in their own garden.

Bible reading/prayer:

O God, you are my God, and I long for you.
My whole being desires you; like a dry, worn-out and waterless land,
my soul is thirsty for you.
Let me see you in the sanctuary;
let me see how mighty and glorious you are.
Your constant love is better than life itself, and so I will praise you.

I will give you thanks as long as I live; I will raise my hands to you in prayer.
My soul will feast and be satisfied, and I will sing glad songs of praise to you.

(Psalm 63:1–5, Good News Bible)

DAY 6

Fact: Washing the car with a hosepipe will waste up to 400 litres or 50 buckets of water. (Source: www.uswitch.com/water)

Challenge: If you wash your car this week, use a bucket of water instead of a hose or a car wash.

Bible reading/prayer:

Wanton waste of water

Wanton waste of water,
thoughtless easy usage,
prideful bonnets gleaming.
Teach us, God our Maker,
to treasure treated water.

Jesus bless our journey,
freeing feckless customs
for your care-filled living.
Inspire us, Holy Spirit,
with planet-healing vision.

Chris Polhill

DAY 7

Fact: By 2080, annual rainfall in the UK will have increased by 11–23%; but rainfall in summer, when demand for water is at its highest, will have decreased by slightly more. (Source: UKCP09 Climate Projections, DEFRA/Met Office)

Challenge: If you have a garden but do not have a water butt to collect rainwater, contact your local council to find out how to obtain one. If you already have one, think of an additional way(s) to collect rainwater.

Bible reading/prayer:

Heal our planet

God our Creator and Healer,
we confess that we have sinned:
we have used creation
not cherished it;
we have lived selfishly
not watched the balance of life;
we have been greedy
not sharing earth's gifts;
and our footprints are heavy
not gentle.

Forgive us the damage
that disturbs our planet.
Grant us the grace
to live for the world's healing
and our own.

Bless the seasons of the year;
may they be restored
to your design.

Chris Polhill

WEEK 6: BIODIVERSITY

DAY 1

Fact: Between 1970 and 1999 the number of sparrows in the UK declined by 62%. Some say this was due to a lack of hedgerows and to changes in farming methods, but in London the figure was a decline of 70% between 1994 and 2000 (Source: British Trust for Ornithology www.bto.org). There are many different theories about why sparrow populations have declined.

Challenge: Arrange to feed birds from October to July (UK). Give them a mix of grain, peanuts and sunflower seeds.

Bible reading/prayer:

Aren't five sparrows sold for two pennies? Yet not one sparrow is forgotten by God. (Luke 12:6, Good News Bible)

DAY 2

Fact: Modern building and farming methods have reduced nesting sites for birds. (Source: Royal Society for the Protection of Birds)

Challenge: Put up a nesting box in a suitable place, such as a garden or churchyard (ask first). Research on the RSPB website (www.rspb.co.uk).

Bible reading/prayer:

'Foxes have holes and birds have nests, but the Son of Man has nowhere to lie down and rest.' (Luke 9:58, Good News Bible)

DAY 3

Fact: Orissa State in India once had more than 1,750 varieties of rice. Now they have only 150. Community seed banks have been set up to try to preserve vital seed. (Source: ITDG/Practical Action). Western food corporations limit biodiversity. In the UK, Garden Organic keeps old varieties of seeds available (www.gardenorganic.org.uk).

Challenge: Count the varieties of apples or potatoes in your local supermarket. Look at labels to see where they were grown.

Bible reading/prayer:

Supermarket blessing

Bless the choices
I will make on this visit
to my local supermarket.

Keep me thankful
for abundant goods
and variety of produce.

Keep me mindful
of your justice
biased in favour of the poor and disadvantaged.

Help me connect
with work of farmers,
the living plants and animals.

Bless the choices
made to keep me living
from this food of your providing.

Chris Polhill

DAY 4

Fact: 40% of species – plants, animals and invertebrates – are sufficiently endangered to be on the IUCN (International Union for Conservation of Nature) Red List of Threatened Species: www.iucnredlist.org

Challenge: Visit a local nature reserve this week.

Bible reading/prayer:

Lord, you have made so many things! How wisely you made them all! The earth is filled with your creatures. (Good News Bible)

DAY 5

Fact: Gardens contain twice as many species as any other habitat type in the UK. The six most widespread bumblebee species are now often more abundant in gardens than in the countryside. (Source: *BBC Wildlife,* Vol. 24, no. 9, p.31)

Challenge: How many days this week have you seen bees flying, and what are they feeding from? Look up some bee-attractors to plant in your garden, or consider having a shelter for mason bees.

Bible reading/prayer:

Serving the hive

As the honeybee lives and works
to serve the queen and the hive,
so may my life serve you this day, Living God,
and the causes of your kin-dom.

Chris Polhill

DAY 6

Fact: Your county council will have a biodiversity plan. See if it is on their website, or phone and ask for a copy. If you have a garden, see how your garden compares with the plan.

Challenge: In your garden or churchyard (ask first) make a small pile of logs/branches to leave to rot.

Bible reading/prayer:

From quark to planet

Creator God,
from quark to planet your universe is awesome.
Give us eyes to gape at the wonders daily about us,
and the will to live in the harmony of your creating.
Help us to own the connections of all things,
even at cost to our own wants and comforts,
so we may live gently on earth,
and all creation praise you. Amen

Chris Polhill

DAY 7

Fact: Mature oaks support a greater number of species than any other tree in the UK, species such as insects and lichen, which is a good indicator of a clean environment. (Sources: BBC Radio; and *The Tree Book*, J. Edward Milner, p.32)

Challenge: Think of five trees you can recognise by the shape of their leaves. Can you see lichen on trees in your neighbourhood? If so, you live in a clean environment.

Bible reading/prayer:

Be glad, earth and sky!
Roar, sea, and every creature in you;
be glad, fields, and everything in you!
The trees of the wood will shout for joy
when the Lord comes to rule the earth.
He will rule the peoples of the world
with justice and fairness. (Psalm 96:11–13, Good News Bible)

God saw everything that he had made, and indeed, it was very good. (Genesis 1:31, NRSV)

EXTRA RESOURCES FOR HOLY WEEK

WEDNESDAY OF HOLY WEEK

Fact: 'A 1 degree Celsius rise [in global temperature], expected by 2020, would see an extra 240 million people experiencing water 'stress' – where supply can no longer be stretched to meet demand.' (Source: Christian Aid)

Today 1.1 billion people still have no access to clean water; and in many parts of the world women and children walk long distances to fetch water for family use. (Source: UNICEF)

Challenge: In solidarity with those who do not have the access to water that we do, fetch all the water for your needs today either from a garden tap or from a co-operative neighbour.

Bible reading/prayer:

Then Jesus poured water into a basin and began to wash the disciples' feet and to wipe them with the towel that was tied around him. He came to Simon Peter, who said to him, 'Lord, are you going to wash my feet?' Jesus answered, 'You do not know now what I am doing, but later you will understand.' Peter said to him, 'You will never wash my feet.' Jesus answered, 'Unless I wash you, you have no share with me.' Simon Peter said to him, 'Lord, not my feet only but also my hands and my head!' Jesus said to him, 'One who has bathed does not need to wash, except for the feet, but is entirely clean. And you are clean, though not all of you.' For he knew who was to betray him; for this reason he said, 'Not all of you are clean.'

After he had washed their feet, had put on his robe, and had returned to the table, he said to them, 'Do you know what I have done to you? You call me Teacher and Lord – and you are right, for that is what I am. So if I, your Lord and Teacher, have washed your feet, you also ought to wash one another's feet.' (John 13:5–14, NRSV)

MAUNDY THURSDAY

Fact: The Kajiado Project in Kenya, run by Practical Action, aims to encourage women to make better use of their donkeys for transport. The project is working with women's groups on promotion of improved donkey-loading practices.

The women have used the time saved from fetching water to cultivate fields and kitchen gardens and attend group meetings; the freeing of time has considerably strengthened the women's groups.

There are now 66 agricultural farms in the village, ranging from 2 to 10 acres, and each of the 43 members of the project has a kitchen garden, in which they grow tomatoes, kale and onions. Members assist each other in their fields and in building their houses. Thirteen new houses have been completed. (Source: Practical Action)

Challenge: Talk to your neighbours today, and find out what they think about environmental issues. You could share some facts you have learned from this six-week challenge.

Bible reading/prayer:

For I received from the Lord the teaching that I passed on to you: that the Lord Jesus, on the night he was betrayed, took a piece of bread, gave thanks to God, broke it, and said, 'This is my body, which is for you. Do this in memory of me.' In the same way, after the supper he took the cup and said, 'This cup is God's new covenant, sealed with my blood. Whenever you drink it, do so in memory of me.' (1 Corinthians 11:23–25, Good News Bible)

GOOD FRIDAY

Fact: 852 million people in the world do not get enough to eat every day. 3 billion people – half the world's population – live in poverty. (Statistics from various NGOs) 'Forget about making poverty history. Climate change will make poverty permanent.' (Nazmul Chowdbury, Practical Action)

Challenge: In solidarity with those who do not get enough to eat, have only one meal today, of grain and vegetables.

Bible reading/prayer:

Nailed!

Nailed!
By disease
that violates, destroys;
by death
that left me lonely;
by poverty
that corrodes the soul;
by war and famine
of the power demand;
by pollution
of a world abused;
by greed; by fear; by rage –
he's nailed!

Nailed by God's will;
as in obedience to love
we live by vocation,
walk into the shadow,
wander with the lost,
following Christ:
God nailed to the cross.

Chris Polhill

EASTER EVE

Fact: Drought, sea-level rise, flooding and storms are all facts of life that poor people are well aware of. But from country to country poor communities tell a story of change – saying that the conditions in recent years are worse than they remember and that the weather is less predictable and more extreme than it used to be.

In Kenya, pastoralist communities are struggling with droughts that have increased in incidence fourfold over the past 25 years. Communities in Honduras face hurricanes that are significantly more frequent and severe than before, even allowing for natural variations. Farmers in Tajikistan have to cope with much hotter summers and changed patterns of rainfall ruining crops and undermining their livelihoods. And in Bangladesh sea-level rise means poor communities have to travel miles every day to collect water as their local well has been contaminated by salt water. (Source: Christian Aid)

Generations-old knowledge about when to sow, plant, restock herds and move to different pastures is rapidly becoming redundant. For people whose entire way of life depends on such knowledge, this is catastrophic

Challenge: In solidarity with the world's poorest people who are now living with the uncertainties and consequences of climate change: after you have cooked your evening meal, put it back in the oven and sit in silence at the dinner table, reflecting on the issues addressed in this Lent Challenge ... Every five minutes, each person rolls a dice; when it is a six, that person gets to eat their meal. For a family, choose beforehand whether to all eat after one person rolls a six, or to wait until everyone has rolled a six.

Bible reading/prayer:

Waiting

Your death, Lord Jesus,
changed everything.
A fearful future
and deep sadness
filled us as we hid.

Gone, the excitement
of being with you.
Challenging confusion,
now lost darkness,
empty misery.

And we wait,
faith, a faint flicker,
hope, a dying ember,
love, a dark flame.
We wait, not knowing
what tomorrow will bring.

Chris Polhill

EASTER DAY

Fact: Practical Action South Asia is developing reliable and cost-effective wind energy systems for charging batteries to help meet the electrical energy needs of rural Sri Lankans who do not have access to the national grid.

For Weerasinghe, a subsistence farmer living in Usgala village in the south of Sri Lanka, being without power was much more than an inconvenience. It was a major source of poverty, preventing him from working, stopping his children from learning, and forcing him to use up precious natural resources – as well as precious hours that could have been spent improving his life instead.

Weerasinghe now generates light from his own small wind turbine system. 'It was wonderful! Straight away there was enough power to light a few light bulbs, so I could work and the children could do their homework. I could charge up my own battery, and earn a little money by charging up those of my friends and neighbours too.' (From Practical Action)

Challenge: Write down something from your personal experience that has been like a resurrection, and share it with a friend.

Bible reading/prayer:

While they were talking and discussing, Jesus himself came near and went with them, but their eyes were kept from recognising him. And he said to them, 'What are you discussing with each other while you walk along?' They stood still, looking sad. Then one of them, whose name was Cleopas, answered him, 'Are you the only stranger in Jerusalem who does not know the things that have taken place there in these days?' He asked them, 'What things?' They replied, 'The things about Jesus of Nazareth, who was a prophet mighty in deed and word before God and all the people, and how our chief priests and leaders handed him over to be condemned to death and crucified him. But we had hoped that he was the one to redeem Israel. Yes, and besides all this, it is now the third day since these things took place. Moreover, some women of our group astounded us. They were at the tomb early this morning, and when they did not find his body there, they came back and told us that they had indeed seen a vision of angels who said that he was alive. Some of those who were with us went to the tomb and found it just as the women had said; but they did not see him.' Then he said to them, 'Oh, how foolish you are, and how slow of heart to believe all that the prophets have declared! Was it not necessary that the Messiah should suffer these things and then enter into his glory?' Then beginning with Moses and all the prophets, he interpreted to them the things about himself in all the scriptures.

As they came near the village to which they were going, he walked ahead as if he were going on. But they urged him strongly, saying, 'Stay with us, because it is almost evening and the day is now nearly over.' So he went in to stay with them. When he was at the table with them, he took bread, blessed and broke it, and gave it to them. Then their eyes were opened, and they recognised him; and he vanished from their sight. They said to each other, 'Were not our hearts burning within us while he was talking to us on the road, while he was opening the scriptures to us?' That same hour they got up and returned to Jerusalem; and they found the eleven and their companions gathered together. They were saying, 'The Lord has risen indeed, and he has appeared to Simon!' Then they told what had happened on the road, and how he had been made known to them in the breaking of the bread. (Luke 24:15–35, NRSV)

AN ACT OF COMMITMENT FOR EASTER DAY
(or for the end of the six-week challenge)

Folk make a commitment to live more in harmony with God's creation by, for example, lighting a candle, planting a seed, writing their name on a paper leaf and hanging it on a prayer tree ... then pray or say together the following words of commitment:

Lord, here I am –
I pledge myself to you
and to this world which you have made.

Here are my ears –
    I pledge myself to listening and learning.

Here are my eyes –
    I pledge myself to never looking away.

Here is my voice –
    I pledge myself to speaking out.

Hear are my hands –
    I pledge myself to getting them dirty.

Here are my feet –
    I pledge myself to walking with care.

Here is my mind –
    I pledge myself to becoming a daring dreamer.

Here is my heart –
    I pledge myself to never give way to despair.

Here is my will –
    I pledge myself to patient perseverance.

Lord, here I am –
    I pledge myself to you
    and to the remaking of our world.

Pat Bennett

ADDITIONAL RESOURCES FOR GROUPS

For each week:

Have a central focus with a candle and objects relating to the week's theme.

Begin by praying one of the prayers or reading one of the Bible passages from the week.

Spend some time sharing together how the challenges have been for everyone during the week.

Discuss:

* What have you found easy in the week's challenge?

* What have you found difficult?

* How can you support and encourage each other with the difficult changes?

* Are there things you can do together? At church? Local campaigns ...?

Keep discussion groups to no more than four people. If you spend all evening on this that would be fine.

Following is additional material for those who need it:

Week 1: Waste

Give some groups Luke 13:18–21 to read, and others Luke 19:1–10.

Consider in your groups what the passage means to you in the light of the environmental crisis we face. Keep the discussion groups to no more than four people, and share in plenary three significant points from your discussion.

End by praying the Lord's Prayer together; hold silence for five minutes after 'your kingdom come', then continue.

Week 2: Consumer choice

Read Luke 12:13–21 together.

Consider what this passage means in the light of the effects of climate change on the world's poorest people. Keep the discussion groups to no more than four people, and share in plenary three significant points from your discussion.

End by praying the Lord's Prayer together; hold silence for five minutes after 'give us this day our daily bread', then continue.

Week 3: Energy

Find a carbon footprint calculator on the Internet; make photocopies for the group. Give people time to fill it in, and then work out your carbon footprints.

Share in small groups what you *feel* about your carbon footprint.

Read meditatively one of the following: Luke 6:37–42; Luke 10:25–37.

End by praying the Lord's Prayer together; hold silence for five minutes after 'forgive us our sins as we forgive those who sin against us', then continue.

Week 4: Transport

Read John 11:1–7 together. You could act this out, with a messenger, Jesus and two disciples, allowing the characters to say more than is in the text: For example, what are the other characters' thoughts and feelings about the conversation?

Consider the pace of life that is experienced by the group. Imagine what your life would be like if you chose only walking as the means of getting from one place to another. Keep the discussion groups to no more than four people, and share in plenary three significant points from your discussion.

End by praying the Lord's Prayer together; hold silence for five minutes after 'your will be done', then continue.

Week 5: Water

Read John 4:1–14 together.

Recall the emotions the media evoke when they report on the environmental crisis. Consider what the Christian faith has to offer to help us with our responses to environmental problems. Keep the discussion groups to no more than four people, and share in plenary three significant points from your discussion.

End by praying the Lord's Prayer together; hold silence for five minutes after 'for the kingdom, the power and the glory are yours', then continue.

Week 6: Biodiversity

Read 1 Corinthians 12:12–27 together.

Consider the interconnectedness of all creation, of which we are a part. Keep the discussion groups to no more than four people, and share in plenary three significant points from your discussion.

Or: Go outside and walk slowly round a garden or natural area and look at the detail of all you see. Share with each other new things that you notice. If you can get hold of a stethoscope, try it on a smooth-barked tree: you should hear something like a heartbeat ...

End by praying the Lord's Prayer together; hold silence for five minutes after 'hallowed be your name', then continue.

Other good resources for groups:

It's Time to Change the Climate, Christian Aid
An Inconvenient Truth, by Al Gore, directed by David Guggenheim, Paramount
Living with the Planet: Making A Difference in a Time of Climate Change, by Catherine von Ruhland, Lion Hudson

ACTION FOR CHANGE:
LITURGICAL RESOURCES

GATHERING RESPONSES

Mother and Father of all life, God-with-us, we gather:
TO BEGIN AGAIN OUR STEWARDSHIP OF YOUR CREATION.

Feed us:
WITH KNOWLEDGE AND UNDERSTANDING.

Awaken within our hearts:
A PASSION FOR SUSTAINABLE LIVING.

Enable us:
TO TAKE LIGHTER FOOTSTEPS ON YOUR GOOD EARTH.

Help us:
TO FIND WAYS OF LIVING MORE SIMPLY.

Stuart Elliott

STRENGTHEN US, MOTHER GOD

Mothering God,
we come to worship
within your renewing love.
So strengthen and encourage us,
that we see the next steps for action,
and have the courage to take them.
For your love's sake.
Amen

Chris Polhill

FREE US FOR ACTION

Each verse and response could be said at a different point in a service.

Loving God, in Jesus you stepped up to the line,
bit the bullet, owned the problem.
Walk beside us as we seek to accept the evidence that the earth is under threat.
Share our pain for the way we have avoided the truth and ignored the signs.
AND FREE US FROM THE GUILT THAT BINDS US.

Loving God, in Jesus you laid yourself open, stuck your neck out,
and made yourself vulnerable to the whims of earthly rulers.
Walk beside us as we risk the consequences of self-examination.
Share our pain for what has been done in self-seeking and blindness.
AND FREE US FROM THE GUILT THAT BINDS US.

Loving God, in Jesus you faced the music,
carried the can, took the blame.
Walk beside us as we seek to accept our part in damaging the earth.
Share our pain for what has been done in foolishness and ignorance.
AND FREE US FROM THE GUILT THAT BINDS US.

Loving God, in Jesus you grasped the nettle, picked up the shovel,
became involved.
Walk beside us as we struggle to change our lives.
Share our pain for what has not been done through fear and weakness.
AND FREE US FROM THE GUILT THAT BINDS US.

John Polhill

A VERSION OF PSALM 16

A: I seek your protection, O God,
    because I am afraid.

B: I long for the good things that come from you
    and I want to follow in your ways.

A: How good it is to be with those who love you,
    what joy their companionship brings.

B: People who put their trust in material things
    will not find satisfaction.

A: I will resist the desire to copy them
    and I reject their values.

B: You, O God, are the foundation of my life,
    I trust my future to you.

A: I praise you for the guidance you have given me
    and because you speak to my conscience.

B: I am constantly aware of your presence,
       so near that I feel safe from harm.

A: This fills me with joy
       and keeps me at peace within myself.

B: You will not leave me, even in my darkest hour;
       and because you love me, I am not alone.

A: You will show me how to live.

B: The sense of your presence
       will be my constant delight.

John Polhill

THE FRIGHTENED MAN WHO COULDN'T SEE

As Jesus was leaving with a great crowd, he passed a man who was frightened and confused because, although he could see that climate change might have disastrous consequences, he was not able to see how to act with confidence of avoiding disaster. So he did nothing.

When he heard about Jesus, he called out to him to have pity on his dilemma. The crowd told him that he should be quiet, because he had made no effort to stop climate change. But he was so frightened that he kept calling out for Jesus to help him.

Jesus stopped and told his followers to bring the frightened man to him. The crowd then began to encourage the man, and he recognised that he should overcome his fear and engage with the issues that troubled him.

Jesus said to him, 'What do you want me to do for you?' The man replied, 'Educate me so that I can see what to do for the best.'

Jesus explained to him how to find information; and when the man had done the research he saw the way to act that fitted Jesus' teaching.

John Polhill

TOWER BLOCK AND COUNTRY COTTAGE

A: I live the high-rise life – and I've got the calves to match! 15 floors up does wonders for fitness.

B: I live in a world of eco-wonder, local-produce heaven – fresh eggs, fresh veg, fresh farmyard smells.

A: My view, 15 floors up? It's a sea of grey, with the edges tinged green; the fields on the horizon tell a distant story.

B: My view: busy veg garden, animals, chickens, from upstairs, a sea of green edged with grey; the town on the horizon, high-risers, a distant story.

A: We are the eco-warriors of this grey world. Away from the hustle of the street, the barking dogs, the unseen wind whistles past; this far up you can almost reach out and touch the land.

B: We know what it means to save the planet, the country way – Slow Food Forever.

A: We're having a one-box, microwave meal, tinged with green: the pre-packed salad on the side, window-box tomatoes dressing the top – less packaging, less water wasted, no time used up; economical, ecological – for us.

B: It's all fresh our supper; takes time to organise however – wash, clean, chickens to the slaughter, veg to steamer; takes time and effort to produce all that.

A: It's not all one-way traffic up this high: what goes up, must come down; your priorities change, the necessity turns to possibility – the possibility of forgetting what you needed on the first trip out!

B: You see, it's where you live that matters ...

A: You see, it's not where you live ...

B: When you live out here the fields are your oysters – well, artichokes, potatoes, carrots ...

A: ... It's your attitude to your *place* ...

B: ... What you make of what you've got, we've got ...

A: ... And we haven't, not that it makes us less aware of our surroundings, what we share, our common land, our inheritance: we all need that piece of green ...

B: ... And some of us need to learn to share it. How many floors up did you say?

A: 15, but there is a lift! We walk it though; it reminds us of the struggle some have to get their food.

Stuart Elliott

HAVE COURAGE TO ACT

Jesus said, 'Daughters of Jerusalem, do not weep for me, but weep for yourselves and for your children … For if they do these things when the wood is green, what will happen when it is dry?' Jesus' words are prophetic, as if on the way to his own death he is able to see all the suffering that is to befall humanity in the ages to come, including all the suffering that humanity is to inflict upon creation.

Ages have passed since that time; our planet is the same size it always has been but with a world population now some sixty times what it was when Jesus walked, stumbling to his cross. For our age – facing a worldwide challenge to life through war, human-induced changing weather patterns, loss of soil fertility and food production – the green wood of God's good earth is truly drying out as planet Earth hots up and competition for resources increases. The cost of not responding to the situation will be very high. Already regions of the earth that once supported viable ecosystems, providing food and shelter for animals and humans, are being abandoned to encroaching deserts or rising sea levels. The innocent are already suffering, and if humanity is to avoid a catastrophe of global dimensions we must act now.

Creation groans as it waits for us to open our minds and hearts to the plight of life. Creation is as much on its way to a Calvary as Jesus was, stumbling and falling on its way to a slow death at our hands. It is still on the way, but thank God we have not yet hammered in the final nails that would seal its fate. There is still time for the green wood of life to regenerate, if we have courage to act.

Simon Davis

FOUND ON THE BEACH
(a reflection from New Zealand)

In the past week, whilst walking along our rocky shore, I have found three pieces of bottle glass, a torn sheet of aluminium from the inside of a refrigerator, a stone adze, a piece of *kauri* (podocarp) tree gum and some interesting rocks.

As I gaze at these objects I think of the bare feet of my grandchildren playing on this beach, and I consider my footprint on God's good earth. The question occurs to me: How do I prepare this land so that those small, bare feet can walk in this valley; and so that the eyes of my grandchildren can see the gift of creation that a loving God has given?

The three pieces of glass and the battered aluminium sheet will be taken to the local community recycling plant. Each year in this way we clean our local beach and sea of corporate pollution, and reuse materials already secured from the surface of our planet.

The *kauri* gum is residue from a natural yearly cycle. However, it is a cycle that is seldom seen now on this island as it requires mature, indigenous podocarps. The sap drips down the bark of the tree and hardens into amber deposits at the base.

Most of the mature podocarps were harvested from this island and removed over a century ago; the timber used to build homes in Auckland and San Francisco. Once the trees were gone, the soil and lumps of gum were washed down the valleys into the sea, where currents brought this piece to our beach.

Each year on this property, we plant three-year-old saplings into the regenerating forest. After five years of planting a number of diverse varieties of saplings, we have twenty-five young *kauri* trees growing towards the canopy. In twenty years' time they will be taller than their shelter trees.

The stone adze is a relic of the first inhabitants of this land. Oral tradition and archaeological record suggests that this area has been occupied since about 1345 CE. The first people to live on this island became known as *Ngati Wai o Aotea*. They were skilled at fashioning stone into weapons, jewellery and tools. Whose hands last held this implement?

The hillsides and high points nearby were long ago fashioned into terraces for defence and gardens. Was this tool part of that work? It fits snugly into my hand.

I, too, work on the slopes of this valley. We need to grow as much fruit and vegetables for our own consumption as we can.

Seaweed from the storms and compost from the kitchen provide rich resource to replenish our clay soils. If the soil is replenished in this way and there is a good supply of water, we have found that we don't need to import commercial fertiliser. Garlic tea seems to repel most creatures who would like to share our crop. The grey and black water from our home is purified on site and returned to the water table.

The interesting rocks speak of thousands of years of sedimentary formation, as well as volcanic outflows and upward forces. The beach contains a conglomeration of different colours and patterns smoothed into increasingly rounded pebbles by the surge of tides and storms.

God, you work over aeons
to fashion smooth stones
on which our children walk.
Others too have walked on these pebbles,
raised children, planted gardens,
    swum and laughed.
May we learn to leave the waters pure,
the slopes blessed with mighty trees,
and the soil vibrant with new life.
For, as we do this
we are acting as stewards of your love,
    expressed in all creation.

Caroline Leys

CONTEMPLATIVE ACTION FOR CHANGE

Many people regard a sense of place as being a prerequisite for effective environmental care and action. When an individual, community or group develops a specific regard for a particular place, this regard is likely to fuel genuine concern and motivation for change in environmental practices.

Regard of this kind has many of the hallmarks of contemplative prayer.

Each place has its own latitude, contours, altitude and angle to the sun. The undulations (or lack of them) contribute to the shape of a watershed. How the water moves towards the sea determines the possibility of pollutants being retained or filtered out by percolation through gravels or wetland. Each activity in the watershed can enhance or impair the quality of the water before it reaches the sea.

The creatures that inhabit a particular location have their own patterns of behaviour. Each delicate interaction between soil, insect, reptile, bird and mammal forms a tapestry that illustrates or denies life.

When you or I form a particular relationship with a place, we could consider this as loving contemplation. Our gaze becomes a form of quiet communion *with* creation. In this process we align ourselves to the quiet or forceful rhythms of creation. As we make ourselves available, we can discover something of the patient and detailed love of God. When this happens we become open to a level of perceptiveness that leads to action.

Action of this kind can simply be removing pollutants in the form of litter. However, it may be more deliberate as we work with neighbours to plant the banks of a local stream with grasses, shrubs and trees native to the region.

We may begin to notice the varieties of birds still visiting the area and ensure that they have natural food sources available during winter or their breeding months.

Local butterflies or bees may rely on the presence of certain grasses or flowering plants for food and energy. Our garden or local park can become a place where space is given over to a wilderness area of suitable plants.

Each of these or other simple actions can be described as acts of loving-kindness.

Caroline Leys

THE RAINFOREST FUND PROJECT

A small group at St John's Methodist Church, Settle, North Yorkshire are concerned about loss of wildlife habitats and species and feel it is a Christian responsibility to look after these for the sake of future generations. We have been raising money for three charities: Two, World Land Trust and Cool Earth, buy up land and give it to a local trust. The third, A Rocha Ghana, works with villagers who live next to Mole National Park.

We have a display in our church hall, which is well used by groups from Settle. So far we have raised £2250. Ways we have raised money are really quite various, including two church coffee mornings, significant donations from individuals, donations from groups that use the hall, small donations in return for use of an Owl electricity monitor, and sponsorship for 'taking old people on nature walks/car trips'.

The loss of habitats and the extinctions that are taking place in our generation are unprecedented. The rainforest absorbs CO_2 and helps to stabilise the climate. To me, these issues seem more important than things like recycling. As little as £50 or £100 can buy an acre of rainforest.

Judith Allinson
http://rainforest-save.blogspot.com

THE EARTHSHIP IN GLASGOW

Milton is a Priority Area Parish in the north of Glasgow. It is a post-war housing scheme, built mainly in the early 1950s, without many amenities – and now even less, with the closure of our two high schools and their facilities.

I came to Colston Parish Church in Milton in the middle of February 2008, and at that point they were already looking at the possibility of a new building, because our present one is falling apart and is woefully inefficient.

At this stage I introduced the idea of an 'earthship': a building made from reclaimed materials, chiefly car tyres, beer cans and glass bottles. A building that is simple and labour-intensive to construct, so allowing lots of unskilled people to join in, and one that is inherently sustainable, being built from reclaimed materials and designed to require minimal, if any, external energy inputs – i.e. it is super-insulated and oriented to the sun to make maximum use of solar gain. And because it can utilise volunteer labour and reclaimed materials it is cheaper to build than a conventional building.

Instantly, the congregation liked the idea, especially getting the community involved and the prospect of a building that would be cheap to construct and even cheaper to run.

At this point it became clear that it was not just a building for the use of the congregation that was needed, but for other groups in Milton too, some of whom use our present building, others who use a community centre due to close, and others who used a Roman Catholic church building recently demolished. So the project grew from being a church building used by the community, to being a community-owned, -built and -run building.

In late September 2008 we received £43,000 from the Climate Challenge Fund of the Scottish government to employ an architect to conduct a feasibility study, a consultation with the community, and to put forward designs for planning permission.

After two months of consultation, we are in the early design stages, looking at site acquisition, and establishing the community vehicle to take the plans forward.

Christopher Rowe

ECO-CONGREGATION

Eco-congregation is an ecumenical organisation that encourages churches to consider environmental issues within a Christian context, and aims to enable churches to make a positive contribution to their life and mission. The use of two eco-congregation study modules – 'Celebrating Creation' and 'Exploring God's Green Word'

– enlivened our group debate. Why celebrate? Why care? Why conserve? These were questions argued and despaired over. Laughter helped. Any disagreement encouraged further investigation. A community sustainability consultant provided some alarming statistics, and our awareness was heightened.

But why choose to discuss global warming in a biblical context, given the magnitude of possible future scenarios? Maybe 'to love God' – and so all God has magnificently provided – required deeper thinking. Maybe 'Love your neighbour as yourself' needed serious application as Bangladesh disappears under the sea, famine grips Africa and resources diminish.

What to do in the face of such distress? Small steps seemed a way forward. Through the local churches, the group would seek an eco-mindset in everything it did. It would consider an energy audit and energy-saving devices; suggest a churchyard survey; look at compost usage. It would consider working with like-minded groups, offering support to community effort and recycling initiatives. It would find out more; seek speakers to be better informed; print eco-advice in the weekly news sheet.

It is said that as St David lay dying he advised his community 'to take care of the little things'. So may we, God willing.

Jennie Juckes, Parish of Llansanffraidi ym Mechain in the Diocese of St Asaph

A FUEL-FREE FLOAT

In August 2005, instead of the usual floats on lorries or on trailers pulled by tractors, the Dunscore Eco-congregation Group decided to have a fuel-free float, highlighting alternative methods of transport. Four people held up bunting to make a 'virtual float' and inside this were members of our group and friends on bicycles and pogo sticks – in wheelbarrows and go-carts. The float also featured our roller-skating minister!

Torrential rain did little to dampen our spirits, and as we travelled to the gala field we sang specially composed songs such as 'There'll be blue skies over the green fields of Dunscore' and 'On an eco-friendly morning' …

Sadly the float did not win a prize, but was fun to do, involved a lot of young folk and was a great talking point.

Matthew Aitken

TUTBURY HYDROELECTRIC PROJECT

Tutbury Mill was constructed in 1781 as a cotton mill, housing 60 carding machines and 7000 spindles. In 1888 the mill was converted into a plaster mill, turning gypsum into 10,000 tons of plaster products. The mill was powered by a man-made watercourse, which is believed to be over a thousand years old and is locally known as Mill Fleam. It was once known as the Little Dove, as it is fed from a weir on the River Dove one kilometre upstream. In its day the mill was capable of producing 750 hp or 560 kW of electricity, which would be enough to supply approximately 500 homes. The mill was demolished in 1968, and British Gypsum gifted the site to the people of Tutbury in 1972.

The site is now a picnic area, including open spaces, playgrounds, a teen shelter and a sculpture relevant to the site.

The flow of Mill Fleam is still in evidence, and, though greatly reduced from its former glory, still supports a variety of wildlife such as fish, herons, kingfishers, bats and more. Downstream there is a project to encourage otters back into the area.

Tutbury Hydroelectric Project aims to reinstate Mill Fleam so that a hydroelectric generator can be installed to generate electricity to be sold off, the proceeds from which will go to the local community and the upkeep of Mill Fleam.

Steve Rhodes

BUTTERFLIES IN CHINA

Can a butterfly in China
start a storm in Aberdeen?

Will the aerosol in London
mean skin cancer in Australia?

Or the car drive to see grandsons
add to hurricanes in America?

We know each nation's carbon
will affect us all someday.
The details may elude us
but our actions all connect.

For this complex living planet
does not know divided nations.

It just needs co-operation
to house human populations.

Chris Polhill

PRAYER STATIONS FOR REFLECTING ON THE BEAUTY AND USE OF PLANET EARTH

Look at the spaces available in the building that you are using. In an average church these will be: space at the back of the church, round the font, in an aisle, in the chancel, near a vestry (or even in one); there may be a side chapel. You may be able to move chairs to create a space. Select your spaces to form a prayer journey round your church.

Define each space using fabric, rope or some natural objects so that it is clear where the station begins and ends.

Have one or more of the following in front of each station: kneelers, prayer stools, one or two chairs, large cushions, a mat.

First station

Place this station in the first space available near the entrance of the church.

Select from these items: a large picture of a beautiful view, a flower arrangement, a small tree branch, stones, postcards of beautiful places, a view of the Earth from space, a globe, pictures of animals, pictures of people looking content or happy, mirrors with biblical phrases taped to them, things like: 'I made you in my image and likeness.' ...

Have a card or board saying, in large print: 'And God saw that it was good.'

Second station

Place this station near the font, or create a font in a suitable space using a large bowl.

Fill the font or bowl with water, and place a container of stones nearby.

Select from these items: a container of rubbish collected from a roadside or a public space; images of war; images of natural disasters, e.g. earthquakes; a number of cards with good intentions written on them (e.g. 'I will use my car less and walk more').

Have a card with baptism promises or one of the baptismal confessions written on it in large print. Have another card inviting people to take a stone (representing the regrets they have for the damage to creation) and to put it in the water. Or invite them to make the sign of the cross on their forehead with the water.

Third station

Place this station in an aisle or other space where normally people would move about.

Have a dead twiggy branch fixed upright, along with green paper, pencils, wool or string, and a hole punch. Invite people to cut out a leaf shape and to write on the leaf actions they are prepared to take, and then (using the hole punch and wool or string) to tie the leaf to the branch.

Have a large board, e.g. blackboard, with a list of things people may already be doing to help creation written on it, with space for people to tick beside each action they are doing or will do.

Have a collection of items like: the fair trade symbol, fair trade food and/or clothes, a veg box, a bike, some carbon footprint calculators ... and paper and pens for people to write a prayer committing themselves to action. Invite folk to take away the carbon footprint calculators.

It is possible to divide this station into three separate prayer stations to invite a more active response.

Fourth station

Place this station in the chancel, chapel or near the usual focus for worship.

Select from these items: a plain cross; candles; heavy dark material; images of where people are suffering because of climate change, e.g. the shrinking of Lake Chad (image on Google); cards with short sentences about the effects of climate change on people in the Third World (see the Christian Aid or Practical Action website); cards with short sentences about the possible changes to the planet depending on the level of global warming; bread and wine.

Invite people to spend time in silence reflecting on these, and then to light a candle as a prayer.

Fifth station

Place this station not far from the previous one, or in a slightly hidden space.

Select from these items: a small Easter garden; cards with stories/facts of where good change is happening (see the Transformation section of this book); a cross of flowers; a low table with small pieces of appropriate rubbish that people can make flowers from and a vase for the flowers; a nest made of clay, moss and sticks; and paper in egg shapes and coloured pens.

Invite people to reflect on their hopes for the planet and community life. They could write their hopes on an egg-shaped piece of paper and place it in the nest. Or they could write a prayer expressing their hopes.

Chris Polhill, based on an idea by Joanna Laynesmith

THAT ALL MAY ACT

Loving God – we pray for the churches.
Grant them insight to perceive that the Earth is at risk.
Grant them a prophetic voice to clarify the actions needed.
Empower your churches to be a model for others.

Living God – we pray for the leaders of nations.
Grant them the vision to see the implications of climate change.
Grant them the wisdom to determine appropriate action
and the conviction to persuade others.

Caring God – we pray for the leaders of our local community.
Grant them time to inform themselves about local environmental issues.
Grant them courage to speak out,
and commitment to see plans through to realisation.

Saviour God – we pray for ourselves.
Grant us hearts that love your creation in all its aspects.
Grant us grace to acknowledge our failure to care.
Grant us compassion for those who will suffer,
and the will to bring about a better and fairer world.

John Polhill

SHOW US HOW TO CHANGE

Show us how to do things well today,
so that others may not suffer,
here or there,
now or in the future.

Show us how to make our contribution
as we change the way we live,
travel, make and consume,
distribute and sell,
use and reuse
energy and products.

Show us how to do simple things well in our home,
places of work and daily lives.
Show us how to protect the world you made,
in all its diversity and goodness,
from our carbon emissions –
global warming and climate change,
rising temperatures and sea levels,
the displacement of peoples, environmental poverty,
harm and destruction.

Show us how and show us why,
so that alone and with others
our contribution will make a difference.
Amen

Robin Morrison

GOD OF HEN AND TIGER

God of hen and tiger,
you number the hairs on our heads
and notice the death of a sparrow.
You gave us qualities of compassion
and concern for the weak.
So feed those qualities in us
by the touch of your Spirit,

that we learn to trust our desire to care
rather than exploit,
and so cherish everything
that you have called into being.

We ask this in the name of Jesus,
who worked tirelessly to bring
healing and peace to those around him.

John Polhill

THE WAY WE LIVE

The way we live
AFFECTS OUR SISTERS,
AFFECTS OUR BROTHERS.

The way we live
AFFECTS OUR PARENTS,
AFFECTS OUR CHILDREN.

The way we live
AFFECTS OUR FRIENDS,
AFFECTS TOTAL STRANGERS.

The way we live
AFFECTS OUR STREET,
AFFECTS OUR COUNTRY.

The way we live
AFFECTS FORESTS AND MOUNTAINS,
AFFECTS RIVERS AND OCEANS.

The way we live
AFFECTS PLANTS AND ANIMALS,
AFFECTS STARS AND PLANETS.

We can choose and change the way we live.
GOD HELP US TO GET THINGS RIGHT.

Ruth Burgess

BLESS US TO LIVE AS YOU CREATED

Bless, O God,
OUR DESIRE TO LIVE SUSTAINABLY.

Bless, O God,
OUR HOPE FOR ALL TO SEE CREATION'S BEAUTY.

Bless, O God,
OUR CARE FOR THE ENVIRONMENT.

Bless, O God,
THE SMALL THINGS WE DO FOR YOUR WORLD.

Bless around us, O God,
THOSE WHO WORK TO BENEFIT YOUR GOOD EARTH.

Bless around us, O God,
THOSE WHO FIND WAYS TO LIVE IN HARMONY WITH CREATION.

Bless us, O God,
THAT WE MAY BE WHOLE AND LIVE AS YOU CREATED US TO BE.

Stuart Elliott

SUSTAINING BLESSING

May the earth sustain your strength,
may Christ sustain your love,
may you sustain one another's joy:
and may you live as a blessing
to God, to the earth and to humanity. Amen

Eleanor Harris

CREATOR GOD, ABUNDANT LIFE YOUR MARK
Tune: Sine nomine ('For all the saints who from their labours rest')

Creator God, abundant life your mark,
you once poured speech into the formless dark
and from those words sprang forth a living spark:
your inspiration – awoke creation.

Throughout this world, in which we live and move,
all that we sense below, around, above
displays the imprint of your longing love:
its revelation – throughout creation.

But yet the earth is fractured, frayed and torn,
poisoned, polluted, ravaged, scarred and worn.
Its treasures plundered and its beauties scorned:
our transformation – of God's creation.

From blight and guilt, we cannot walk away.
Our will and actions shape the world today
and ours the greed, insisting on its way,
whose depredations – despoil creation.

Come, Holy Spirit, challenge mind and heart!
Inspire our living so that we will start
to make those choices which may yet impart
love's liberation – to your creation.

We pledge to touch all things with holy care
until your coming Kingdom ends despair.
Then all the world will witness and will share
the jubilation – of healed creation.

Pat Bennett

STARTLE US, GOD, BY THE SIGNS OF YOUR SPIRIT
Tune: Lobe den herren (Praise to the Lord, the Almighty)

Startle us, God, by the signs of Your Spirit around us!
Shake us awake for the thrust of Your word to astound us!
    Rattle our doors,
    give our discomfort no pause,
rouse us for work You have found us!

Wake us to see where the winds of the city are blowing,
facing the brokers of power where the currents are flowing,
    finding the lost,
    learning what justice may cost,
feeling the pain of our growing.

Shock us by showing us Jesus, his style of direction,
welcoming, never conventional in his selection;
    open our minds,
    teach us how prejudice blinds,
colours our culture's reflection.

Startle us, God, into confident high expectation,
knowing the hope and the promise of new revelation,
    taking Your part,
    praising with mind and with heart,
honouring all Your creation.

Shirley Erena Murray

THE STRUGGLE TO CHANGE

THE STRUGGLE TO CHANGE

Human beings have always brought about change through struggle. Debate tests the validity and strength of concern, until more people are convinced that the proposed changes are the better way forward. Struggles can be destructive; they can also bring about justice and creative change. The Christian way is focussed on the will of God in the sure knowledge that God loves us and walks beside us, though discerning and agreeing God's will for particular issues can be a struggle all its own. The environmental challenges that face us will need radical change, but we have brought about change before.

In the 1960s and 70s those who were campaigning on environmental issues were by and large concerned with local effects of pollutants: poor air quality, contaminated rivers and ground. Due to their activism, and the influence it has had on governments, there has been a very marked improvement in these areas, at least in developed Western countries. Christian groups have been very much involved in these changes, and the work of such groups needs to be acknowledged and celebrated. However, in recent years the emphasis has changed; we now face much wider issues concerning the sustainable future of the planet: the need to ensure a sufficient level of biodiversity so that none of the essential interactions between different parts of the natural world are compromised; the need to preserve existing energy sources and to develop new, cleaner sources that can provide for our children and grandchildren. And over all these issues we have the overwhelming fact of accelerated climate change. The current best prediction by the international scientific community is for a rise in average global temperatures of between 2 and 4 degrees Celsius over the next 60 or 70 years. These predictions are based on complex computer models of the Earth's atmosphere, and the different models used in different countries are all broadly consistent in the temperature rises they predict – and are all in agreement that most of this change is anthropogenic, or, in simpler terms, is being caused by human activity and the production of greenhouse gases such as carbon dioxide – and in particular by the use of fossil fuels in industry, in transport and in our homes. The effects of a two-degree global temperature rise will be difficult enough to cope with – with failing crops, particularly in the developing world; a decrease in water availability in many parts of the world; an increase in extreme storms; and the loss of much natural habitat, with consequent species extinction. A four-degree temperature rise would be catastrophic – with crop failures and water shortages around the world; the flooding of many major cities and populated areas due to sea-level rise; the mass extinction of species; and the possibility of major climatic instabilities. All these changes can be expected to lead to the mass migration of whole communities, with all the possibilities for conflict that that holds.

So faced with such scenarios, how should Christians react? It would be relatively easy to list at this point all the small and large things that individuals could do that might in some way reduce these effects. Governments and industry, too, need to know that they have our support for the changes they must make. However, it is worth considering these issues briefly from a theological perspective. There seem to be four principles that are worth considering.

We are called in scripture to be 'gardeners'. The creation story is of course set in a garden, over which Adam and Eve were given responsibility. It is no accident that the story of the new creation of Jesus' resurrection is set in a garden. So perhaps we could consider how we can be gardeners of God's good creation, in terms of care for the environment around us; its responsible use for the provision of food; and in making it a place of beauty in which all may find peace.

Jesus summarises all his teaching in his call to love our neighbours as ourselves, and this principle of neighbour love is central to the life and worship of the church. Trying to be clever, a listener asked Jesus precisely who was his neighbour; and of course this led Jesus to tell the story of the Good Samaritan, the hated foreigner who tended the beaten Jew. In our globalised age, this parable surely suggests we should interpret Jesus' call to neighbour love in the widest possible terms – to all on this planet of ours now, and in the years to come. This then leads us to reflect: How can we show such love to those whose countries are being eaten away by sea-level rise and to those whose crops are failing ever more frequently? Reflect, too, on how we can be peacemakers when scarce resources need sharing, populations are moving, and fear for survival pushes justice to the margins. Governments need to know that they have our support for the international co-operation that is a necessary part of this struggle to restore the balance of the environment. Such considerations might well cause us to be a little uncomfortable about our Western lifestyle, which is profligate in the use of energy and in the production of greenhouse gases.

In the Sermon on the Mount, Jesus talks of his people being 'salt of the earth' and 'light to the world', and it is clear that we are called to witness to his presence with us in the way that we live our lives. Yet often our lifestyles are more or less indistinguishable from the lifestyles of those around us. Jesus' followers are called to a prophetic role – by their words and actions to make the way of God clear. But to be a prophet involves sacrifice of our own ambitions and desires, and can easily lead to scorn and persecution. If we are to fulfil such a role, and proclaim the message of neighbour love, it is quite possible that we may follow our Lord along the Via Dolorosa.

While these thoughts and reflections are serious and disturbing, as Christians we do have hope. The hope that, with God beside us, we can engage with the present struggle in a life-giving way that will bring healing change – the Acts of the Apostles shows us a group of ordinary people who, with God's help, do extraordinary things. St Paul, in talking of the resurrection hope and this new creation in his letter to the Corinthians, tells us that all our work will not be in vain. All that we do to protect and beautify God's world, however small, will find its place and fulfilment in that new creation. Every act of justice and mercy and love that we perform will be honoured and preserved.

Reflecting on these themes may well lead each of us to quite different ways of responding and acting – inevitably so, as God's plan for each of us is different and unique. The prayers and worship resources that follow allow us to reflect on these thoughts, and no doubt many others, and to hear God's voice speaking to each of us. Before Jesus embarked on a number of crucial phases in his ministry we find him in prayer – most notably in the Garden of Gethsemane. May these prayers that follow be the starting points for the way that Jesus has set before us, however hard that way might be; but may we walk that way knowing the hope of the resurrection and the new creation in our hearts.

Chris Baker

THE STRUGGLE TO CHANGE:
LITURGICAL RESOURCES

TOGETHER WE STRUGGLE

Here together, we bring our struggle for change.
PRAISE GOD WHO NEVER LEAVES US.

Here together, we own our connection with all things.
PRAISE GOD WHO WALKS BESIDE US.

Here together, we listen for God's word.
PRAISE GOD WHO DAILY INSPIRES US.

Here together, we pledge ourselves to action.
PRAISE GOD WHO WRESTLES ALONGSIDE US.

Chris Polhill

JESUS OUR MODEL

Living God, we praise and thank you
for the gift of Jesus
as a model for human life.
As we seek to mould ourselves on that pattern, we recall:
his encounter with men who would stone a woman,
his feeding of the five thousand,
his arguments with the Pharisees.

Walk with us, as we struggle
to find ways to resolve conflict,
to share scarce resources,
and to realise peace with justice
in the world, and all the places of our lives.

John Polhill

COLLECT FOR CREATIONTIDE

Creator God,
whose Son Jesus Christ lived once in Palestine,
yet whose arms flung wide on the cross,
embrace all time and space in redeeming love.

Grant that we, living here and now,
may plant and water the new garden of the Lord
throughout the earth and for generations to come;
by the power of the sustaining Spirit. Amen

Eleanor Harris

CHALLENGE US TO THINK AGAIN

God of creating love, we give thanks for this beautiful world you have created.
We give thanks in celebration of all its diversity and fragility.
In your generosity you have lent it to us to care for it, nurture it and love it.
Thank you for that constant generosity.

God of humanity, we give thanks for all your people,
for our diversity, intensity and difference.
We celebrate the brightness and colourfulness of your people.
Thank you for creating us in such variety.

God of purpose, you knew the plan and purpose for it all,
yet, Lord, somewhere along the road things have gone wrong.
Parts of creation's beauty have gone sour,
people have become possessive and greedy.
Was this your plan, Lord God?
We know we have gone very badly wrong.

Forgiving God, you set us a challenge to care for your world,
yet sadly, we have abused it in so many ways.
Your people are suffering and broken,
nature has been pushed too far,
almost too far to survive,
all because of our greed and desire for bigger and better.

Weeping God, you must weep heavy tears.
Forgive us, God. Forgive us.

Silence

Challenge us daily to look at our thoughts, words and actions.
CHALLENGE US TO THINK AGAIN.

Challenge us daily to look beyond our own wants and needs to the needs of others
and of this world.
CHALLENGE US TO THINK AGAIN.

Challenge us to be strong, for you and for our brothers and sisters in the world.
CHALLENGE US TO ACT IN YOUR NAME.
AMEN

Biddy Crossfield

GOD OF COMPASSION, HEAL US

Leader: God of history and hope,
        we offer to your forgiving love the sins of our common past:
A: The arrogance that took another's land.
B: The greed which plundered resources.
A: The national pride which diminished others.

Silence in which to offer the sin in our personal history …

Leader: O God of compassion,
ALL: HEAR OUR SORROW AND HEAL US.

Leader: God of power and weakness,
        we offer to your forgiving love our abuse of both our power and our weakness:
B: The use of military might to force our will on others.
A: The unbalanced sharing of the earth's resources.
B: The weaknesses that prevent us insisting on justice.

Silence in which to offer the sin of the misuse of our personal power and weakness …

Leader: O God of compassion,
ALL: HEAR OUR SORROW AND HEAL US.

Leader: God of sacrifice and gift,
        we offer to your forgiving love the selfish materialism of our common life:
A: The economic system demanding spending and debt to sustain it.
B: The wasteful use of the gifts of your creation.
A: The desire for more that is never satisfied.

Silence in which to offer the sin of our personal selfishness …

Leader: O God of compassion,
ALL: HEAR OUR SORROW AND HEAL US.

Leader: God of heaven and earth,
        we offer to your forgiving love the damage we are doing to this planet:
B: The atmospheric changes caused by fossil fuels and chemical fumes.
A: The melting ice of sea and glacier that threatens flood and desert.
B: The disappearing species lost through climate change.

Silence in which to offer our personal struggle …

Leader: O God of compassion,
ALL: HEAR OUR SORROW AND HEAL US.

Leader: The Living God offers us the gifts
        of love and forgiveness,
        renews our hope and
        inspires our vision.
ALL: THANKS BE TO GOD. AMEN

Chris Polhill

A VERSION OF PSALM 18

A: How I love you, O God:
      you are the source of my strength,
      my safety, and my confidence.

B: You are the place I retreat to,
      my protection from danger;
      you care for me in times of difficulty.

A: When I was in desperate need
      I asked you for help.
      You were there at my side,
      you understood what I needed.

B: I felt that I was being rescued,
      hoisted up out of a raging torrent.

A: Brought to a safe house
            where I would be loved.

B: You will bring me to life, O God;
            you will shine a light in my darkness.

A: With you I feel able to overcome any difficulty,
            to leap over any obstacle.

B: When I have a sense of your will for me,
            I feel able to act with confidence
            and without fear.

A: Nothing and no one is able to give me such strength,
            such confidence to step out into the unknown.

B: When I listen to your voice
            the way ahead seems clear
            and everything falls into place.

A and B: God is with me, and is everything to me –
            I cannot contain the joy that I feel.

John Polhill

QUESTIONS

To fly or not to fly? – that is the question:
whether it is better for the planet to risk
damp greyness of a British summer,
or to take the plane travelling to distant shores;
so in bright warmth relax – meet Thai, meet African,
no more? To support a poorer culture
with the need to take a break,
and by my holiday learn more of them.
'Tis surely better than a walled hotel
of Western pleasure on The Gambia's shore?
But what of carbon? Ah! There's the rub.
An element when burned
rises through the sky to make a thicker blanket,
a stratum in the atmosphere

to warm the seas and change the weather,
throwing all in flux.
What then for all – let alone the hapless poor?
Useless the ancient knowledge of seedtime and harvest,
seasons of rain and sun, all is change, all uncertain.
We here do sleep, perchance to dream
of times when we knew naught of such a harm,
building still e'en larger places for the plane,
when it doth burn its fuel higher in the skies
than any other form of travel that we know.
How now can we ignore it – commerce and travellers both?
Yet how shrink back within our little shores?
Time marches onwards never back.
Let conscience give us courage to move forwards,
our native resolution strengthen us to find gentle ways
for our world's enterprises of great moment.
Meanwhile, dear friends, till these are found
we could consider this adventure
that we will travel on the ground.

Chris Polhill *(with apologies to Shakespeare)*

CREATION, THE FIRST CATHEDRAL

'We're all going to die.' And that is why, maybe, many do not worry about the Green-land glaciers shedding into the Atlantic. All the self-sacrifices would be a lot of effort for no gain, since the gains benefit the next generation, whereas we have to bear the cost. José Maria Figueres Olsen, former President of Costa Rica and former Chief Executive Officer of the World Economic Forum, said: 'You know when people built the cathedrals, they behaved as if they could see them completed in one generation, though it was the work of many generations. So is the fight against climate change.'

What use is an empty cathedral? Cathedrals are built to fill us with awe and wonder, to bring praise to our lips and a song to our hearts. Creation is the first of all cathedrals – it dazzles and amazes us, causing us to praise and sing.

When through the carelessness or selfishness of humanity creation is dimin-ished, when a creature or plant becomes extinct, it is like chipping a piece off a cathedral. At first such a small piece missing is not noticed. In time, as piece by piece disappears, the appearance of the cathedral is changed. In time whole parts may become unstable, threatening to fall in, letting in the elements and hastening the day when the whole building crumbles into ruin.

The Cathedral of creation is a dwelling that needs all its parts, designed by the Architect of life. God calls us to walk around and within creation, to wonder at its complexity and beauty, so that from wonder might spring afresh our ancient vocation to tend and bless the gift of life.

Simon Davis

THE CROSS OF CREATION

We are crucifying creation.
Look! See, in Christ's blood poured out –
the extinction of the planet's species,
the richness and diversity of life
depleted and diminished.

In the muscles and sinews of the Christ,
straining against the cross,
the stress of ecosystems, breaking down,
the ozone layer depleted and
global climate changes.

The nails – work of human hands –
our technology,
pinning down the movement of living creatures,
asphyxiating life through pollution,
killing the forests and its creatures.

The crown of thorns,
brutal use of creation by human hands:
where the poor suffer most
and the rich are protected.
Did we unwittingly cry: 'Crucify him!'?

Christ looks from the cross.
'Behold,' he says, and changes relationships.
Behold creation, its suffering and pain,
and see it as a family
worth our struggle to change.

Simon Davis and Chris Polhill

GREEN MARTYRS

Our Celtic Christian ancestors were not satisfied with only one form of martyrdom, that of dying for your faith through another's aggressive action. They called those who died this way red martyrs, but went on to develop two other kinds of martyrdom which you could choose to undertake. One was white martyrdom. This was where, for the sake of the gospel, you left all that was known to you of family place and clan and travelled to where the Spirit directed you and stayed there, living the gospel and teaching it. The third was green martyrdom. This was to undertake a difficult prayer, like praying in the sea.

The sacrifices and changes we undertake for the sake of the environment are often hard and can put us out of step with our neighbours. The prayer we make to change our hearts for the sake of creation is difficult. The idea of green martyrdom can help us with this.

The charter below was developed on a week at Iona Abbey. Feel free to amend it or add to it.

As green martyrs, we aim to pursue a way of life that minimises our individual impact on the environment. When making lifestyle choices, we value concern for the environment above considerations of cost, convenience and personal comfort.

Lifestyle choices include:
- Frequency, distance and mode of transport
- Source, production process and delivery distances of food and other products
- Consumption of electricity, gas and other energy sources
- Waste creation and product re-use
- Having respect for all living things

Concern for the environment means:
- Preserving in harmony the natural habitats of all life-forms
- Not compromising the resources available to future generations of all species
- Sharing scarce resources equitably

Where a choice may lead to higher cost or loss of convenience and personal comfort to:
- Be aware of our personal limitations
- Take delight in our ability to make choices that protect creation
- Stop, think, pray, and choose

Members of the Practical Celtic Spirituality Week led by Chris and John Polhill,
Iona Abbey, 2006

WHAT IN THE WORLD CAN BE DONE?

An international problem demands an international solution. Small, individual actions are the right thing to do, but the belief that they are making any major impact on a global phenomenon is misguided. In the UK, for example, carbon emissions amount to 2% of the world's total; an individual or small percentage of the 60 million population acting greenly at home is only going to make a negligible difference to the planetary whole.

However, by uniting with others via conservation and environmental groups and campaigning for change at national and international levels, great strides can be made. Authors Mark Lynas and James Lovelock make considered proposals for national and international campaigns in their respective books on climate change.* A country like Britain, for example, which is especially influential as a member of the G8 group of industrialised nations, can encourage development and innovation in alternative energies and technologies, and export that expertise to countries with fast-growing economies such as China and India, which are overproducing greenhouse gas emissions.

Catherine von Ruhland, from *Living with the Planet: Making a Difference in a Time of Climate Change*

* *See* High Tide: How Climate Crisis Is Engulfing our Planet, *by Mark Lynas, and* The Revenge of Gaia: Why the Earth Is Fighting Back – and How We Can Still Save Humanity, *by James Lovelock*

BECOMING A VEGAN

I became a vegan because the thought of treating a living, sentient organism as a machine, with the purpose of sustaining humanity, seemed to me to be wrong. There is no ethical problem with eating meat per se, to my mind, but as part of an industrialised system, we have come to see everything as automata, to our detriment and theirs.

I have done well out of industrialisation; indeed, I owe my life to it. But so does much of the burgeoning population. Without industrialisation, we would certainly not be able to coax the environment into sustaining a population of more than six billion. And as that population grows richer, meat, which is seen as a luxury food, is more in demand. Grain and water, which could feed millions of people, are instead used to feed millions of animals, who are then used to feed rather fewer people.

Eating socially as a vegan, in restaurants or in people's homes, would be difficult, I thought – I would have to make a very un-British nuisance of myself. Also, I have to travel as part of my work, but having been a vegetarian for ten years I had already struggled with that abroad. I sometimes feel it is bad manners to ask other cultures to bow down to my dietary whim. I was also addicted to cheese, and very much enjoyed a scrambled egg from time to time. To be honest, it was this last issue that proved the chief obstacle to veganism in my case.

At home, being a vegan proved surprisingly easy, not least because my partner is also vegan. I found a cheese substitute that I now prefer to the real thing. Other than that, it was simply a case of learning which products had ingredients derived from animals (it is surprising how many do) and either doing without them or finding an alternative. I haven't noticed any nutritional deficiency, but I do take the occasional 'paranoid' vitamin and mineral supplement (plenty of non-vegans do the same, however). Eating out is more difficult. Some restaurants are really helpful and, locally at least, you get to know which they are. Most of my friends are vegetarian, or vegan themselves, which means that visiting has not really been a problem.

Travelling has proved more challenging. It is often stressful enough, without worrying about diet. I have therefore allowed myself to be vegetarian when abroad. However, this has not always been necessary. In Japan, there is a Buddhist monks' cuisine called *shojin ryori,* which happens to be vegan, and this gave me an opportunity to experience a part of their culture without a whiff of imperialism. The Internet has also proved helpful. A very useful website called 'Happy Cow' directed me to a lovely vegetarian restaurant in Brussels, where I was able to get a delicious vegan meal. At conferences there are often several vegetarians and this can help to break the ice, particularly as organisers tend to group all the vegetarians together for the benefit of the caterers at mealtimes.

I do crave eggs and cheese sometimes. I even find myself drooling at the thought of a juicy steak. I often get bored of explaining the reasons why I made the choice I did, and if I were paid every time someone told me they don't eat much meat, I'd be considerably wealthier, and probably wouldn't mind so much. For all that, I am happier being a vegan, and the discipline proved much less of a struggle than I thought it would.

Gary Polhill

GOING CARBON NEUTRAL STIRLING

We all have an idea of what kind of community we would prefer to live in. Many of us have some understanding of the global environmental problems that affect us all. Sadly, few of us actually feel empowered to make the changes that we would like to see in our communities, and it is all too common a belief that individuals and small groups do not have a big enough influence to affect what is happening to our global environment.

This is why Going Carbon Neutral Stirling was set up. We know that people have genuine goodwill and we wanted to show them that they – not only politicians – can make a huge difference to their own communities, and by doing this, they will have a significant positive effect on the global environment.

As our name suggests, we look at the problem of carbon emissions in Stirling. Our team have the task of getting people to recognise the problem, without looking for a scapegoat. We go to local community groups and work with different people according to their needs, showing them what can be done and what benefits they will gain by coming together and making changes to how they live and work. The changes can be quite simple – for example, making short journeys on foot instead of by car – but added up they will make a big difference to a person's carbon footprint, and each individual's action will combine to have a massive positive impact on the environment. Businesses too are being shown how they can benefit from looking at changing the way they operate – after all, our shops and offices are part of the wider community and must feel that they can do something to be part of the solution.

One of the most difficult struggles is to get people to face up to the problems they might encounter in their community, instead of turning away from them. Once they find that other people want to join in and work with them, things are easier, but the initial step is sometimes a struggle. This is probably because once you acknowledge something is wrong, you then feel some responsibility for doing something about it, but alone this can be very daunting – and there's always the possibility that you might fail. It's much simpler to ignore a problem. It can be difficult to muster up courage in order to do the right thing on your own, but with others it becomes possible.

GCNS is a true grassroots project which guides and empowers the community to act. From our feedback so far, we can see that individuals are beginning to look outwards towards their whole community far more and are becoming more involved in what is going on around them. Over time, the benefits of making consumption reductions become clear and these benefits are ultimately far greater than what has been given up. We are all given back the possibility of a future where people realise the true value of a good community and the importance of being aware of the environment.

Clare Speedie

AN ECO-JOURNEY

I must have been very bored one evening in 2003 when I attended a workshop at church on waste disposal, held by our local council, as, let's be honest, it doesn't exactly sound like a particularly exciting evening's entertainment, does it?

Little did I know where it would lead! I was definitely not an eco-warrior or tree hugger – nothing could have been further from my mind. That evening, however, I was introduced to the concept of individual environmental responsibility and heard about Eco-team: a supported programme using a workbook, the aim of which was to help households to reduce their impact on the environment, with measurable reductions in waste, energy and water. Those of us from church who completed the Eco-team course felt at the end that instead of a finishing point, we were facing a beginning. We all believed strongly that we now had this awakening awareness of human impact on the earth alongside a developing knowledge base of what each of us could do to make a difference, and we wanted to share it with others.

When we heard about the Eco-congregation programme, it seemed like the ideal way to move forward at church. We approached our minister, church elders and church members for permission to do a church environmental audit and to follow up with appropriate actions. We were encouraged by enormous support and six of us went on to form Reigate Park Church Eco-team, and in 2007 we achieved our first Eco-congregation Award.

We had looked at three areas of church life – practical, spiritual and community – and chose actions within those areas that were easy to achieve or that we felt passionately about. Examples of the many actions included putting in place recycling facilities at church, developing an information leaflet about recycling facilities in our area, running a creation care Bible study, and running a 4-day Environmental Easter workshop for 120 primary school children.

It hasn't all been plain sailing though. We have faced, and continue to face, many blocks to progress – and rightly so, for it forces us to be quite certain of our facts and to be able to justify why we want to make changes. The blocks have tended to fall into one of four categories: lack of time, financial, apathy or disbelief. For instance, I shall never forget the thirty-something family man, who had just bought an

£800,000 house, saying that he couldn't afford to buy a water butt. Or the man who felt we were wasting our time, as we couldn't possibly make any difference to this dreadful global disaster. The way we have tackled these situations is to always keep being positive, never judgemental and to keep educating people, and ourselves, in many different ways. Our motto has always been: 'Alone we can make great changes, and together we can save the world!'

Almost 7 years later, and most members of the initial Eco-team have moved on. There was a difficult transition period, when it felt as if momentum and interest was waning, but it was a necessary process to go through, so that others in the church could come forward and take on the challenges that are now owned by the whole church rather than a select group. Caring for the environment is still a core principle of our church. An environmental church action plan has been developed and progress is reported on annually at a church meeting. We still share our passion for caring for the world, both in church and in the local community as we take school assemblies, run school eco-lessons and lead eco-workshops at other churches and community groups. A member of the Eco-team has completed a Master's degree in plant ecology and I now write a monthly column on eco-issues for my Church's national magazine. What a journey it has been!

Sonia Christie, Reigate Park Church

CONTROVERSY AND COMPROMISE

Abbotsford Parish Church became an eco-congregation in 2006. We had numerous activities already underway, e.g. recycling of spectacles, phones and printer cartridges, and strong links with community organisations. We also had our tree: a stylised, two-metre-high wooden silhouette. This was the focus for our worship space for a year, changing with the seasons. However, whilst few objected to seeing it decked with eco-pledges, and with cardboard flames at Pentecost, there were a few raised eyebrows when it blossomed red poppies on Remembrance Sunday, some muttered comments when it was painted black and stripped to just two branches at Easter – and voluble protests when it supplanted the traditional conifer at Christmas. As a compromise, a 'real' Christmas tree was bought and set up in the church hall.

This combination of controversy and compromise sums up Abbotsford's eco-story. We're hugely fortunate to have a minister who is 100% eco-friendly and a couple of environmental scientists on our Green Team, who know about things like climate change. However, the wider congregation still remain divided: for every eco-apostle, there's an eco-cynic who considers green issues irrelevant, or someone who feels that it isn't the role of the church to get involved in such matters.

So we tread lightly, trying to encourage wide participation and build things up just a little at a time. And it's working. We had a visit from the Energy Saving Trust and, as a result, we're now fitting an optimiser to increase the energy-efficiency of our boiler. Our sanctuary will soon have low-energy lighting, thanks to funds raised by the Green Team. Occasional eco-liturgy has developed into a whole month of eco-services, starting with Harvest and ending with 'BioMass', an all-age communion with an environmental theme. And when local urban regeneration project Clydebank Re-Built offered to provide lighting for our church tower, many of the congregation pledged to switch to low-energy light bulbs in their homes to offset the extra energy that would be used.

Christine Davidson

GREENING OUR BUILDINGS

We have just finished a major reordering at Christ Church, Chislehurst. We completely renovated our 1907 hall and built a two-storey extension to the west; and we've joined the hall to the adjacent 1897 church to the south. The three key eco-features are:

1. The insulating of existing walls (as well as, of course, the new-build walls). Benefits: less heat loss. Drawbacks: none we can think of.

2. The harvesting of grey water for toilet flushing. Benefits: less processed water being used. Drawbacks: the pump, which brings the grey water from storage, uses electricity – but it is difficult to gauge how much, so we'll never know whether the carbon emissions we're producing by using this electricity are more or less than those we would have created by processing the mains water we would otherwise have used.

3. The drilling of boreholes to tap geothermal heat, which we then pump under the floor of the new-build to heat the new areas. Benefits: we were told by the engineers that the carbon emissions would be 20% less (and that the heat would cost about £200 a year less) than had we heated these areas by conventional gas boilers (though we have no way of proving it since they're new areas we haven't had to heat before). Drawbacks: Estimated to have cost £60,000 more to install than traditional heating, but we were given a government grant of £17,000.

Christopher Scott, Christ Church, Chislehurst, Kent, 2008

GIVING UP THE CAR

'No,' I said, quite firmly to the council employee, who, let's be fair, was just "doing her job". 'We won't have a car.'

'So how are you going to get your children to the school we have offered you then?'

'That's the point, that school is no good, it is too far away.'

'No, it is within the statutory limit.'

I was beginning to lose patience – this had already gone on for quite some time!

'No, it is *on* the statutory limit. And you don't expect us to walk our children to school, you expect us to drive them: that being the whole point – we won't be able to!'

This was the first battle we fought over not having a car. I had to attend a tribunal at the council and state my case for wanting a closer school. It did help that the council had really messed up our application.

We had moved from a really rural area – tracks, mud and mountains – to a city with good public transport and bad city-centre parking. The cost of keeping a car that would be idle much of the time made no sense.

It surprised me how quickly I got used to not having a car, and how many people wondered how, with two children, we were going to cope without one! Actually it was quite easy: we had discovered the bus network, and the local trains were also frequent and close. Shopping was a challenge. Although we had a local Spar shop just around the corner, there was a huge expanse of shopping heaven (or hell) about a mile away, and so, armed with rucksacks, we shopped there. Then we started to discover other places.

There were little rows of shops all around us; the kind you find in any large urban area. Local shops were easier and far better to go to. Our local park was on the way to the butcher, veg shop, fancy cheese shop for treats, all mostly local produce which we did not find in supermarkets. In another direction there was a great French deli; in another, a local co-op great for the groceries that couldn't be bought anywhere else. We developed a network of routes throughout the area. Library and co-op were close-by so those trips were amalgamated. Park and butcher's and Bronwen's house (a friend of our daughters) …

Time was spent very differently: Rather than finding somewhere to go, then driving there, we would select an area, then go and see what it had to offer. Time spent travelling as a family was relaxing. It was a time for nothing else but to be together, and to enjoy the journey. And we weren't in control of the vehicle, so couldn't get cross.

After a year or so, the world had shrunk a bit. Getting to something 20 miles away needed planning. Those places that were not on bus or train routes (and too far to cycle) were like unknown lands on old maps (here be dragons!). The only time we really missed the car was when the hospital was needed urgently. However, having immersed ourselves in the local community, a neighbour stepped in and helped. We even had the offer (which we took up on a few occasions) of the free loan of a car through the Greenbelt Generous Network.

I never did understand the mentality that says: 'house to car, to work, to car, to house without seeing the bits in between'. There were frustrations, but we appreciated our local community far more by not having a car than we would ever have done as motorists.

Stuart Elliott

THE DI LEMMAS

The Di Lemmas are a family of life-sized cardboard puppets, created, dressed and operated by the children and young people in our church. We came up with the idea of the Di Lemmas as a teaching and discussion tool that could be used on an ongoing basis in a variety of church settings – from worship to a Green Fair.

The key point is that this particular family holds diverse points of view within it: they regularly face ethical choices of all kinds, and they often disagree on the way ahead. But they do love and respect each other, and want to find workable solutions that both honour their faith and keep the family together. All, unsurprisingly, just like our church!

To set up possible disagreements on eco-issues, and to encourage imaginative solutions to real eco-problems, we named each member of the Di Lemma family carefully, assigning personalities that suggest distinctive (though not entirely predictable) angles: Father = Eco, Mother = Heerza, Boy = Sticky, Girl = Constant, Grandmother = Solva. They are of mixed international experience and have a wealth of skills between them.

One time we used the Di Lemmas to explore the serious challenge of international air travel. Called 'Love

Miles', our invented scenario involved a family wedding in India, with an elderly grandfather there who wanted to see his grandchildren (Sticky and Constant), presenting the almost impossible choice for the Di Lemmas of whether to go or not. Well, Eco had no doubts whatsoever – he was totally against it, proving that the most 'far-thinking' people can also sometimes be the most rigidly narrow. In the end, after much discussion and research, with Solva's wisdom and the children's ability to explore the Internet – and with input and suggestions from our congregation – the Di Lemmas *did* go to India, but by a very unusual route …

Leanne Langley, Avenue St Andrew's United Reformed Church, Southampton

THE WIND FARM DRAMA

A: Nimby.

B: What?

A: Nimby!

B: Who are you calling a Nimby?

A: You, N-I-M-B-Y. Not In My Backyard.

B: Your backyard? What's not in your backyard?

A: It's what's going to be in *your* backyard, you Nimby!

B: Oh, I suppose you are referring to the new wind farm on our beautiful hills, which will irreparably alter the landscape for good, changing the view that we have had forever and making our village unfit to live in.

A: Sorry?

B: Oh never mind, you eco-types never will understand the beauty of the natural landscape – the view that is about to be lost forever!

A: Natural landscape? Half of those hills wouldn't be there without the mines … And the cultivated fields are hardly a natural –

B: Sorry, I don't see what this has got to do with the wind farm ruining our picturesque view.

A: Never mind ... Can I ask you something?

B: OK, what?

A: How much electricity do you use?

B: Eh? Oh, I don't know really. I suppose about the normal amount!

A: I see, normal for whom? Do you leave your TVs on standby, mobile phones plugged in, computers switched on, use the drier instead of a washing line ...?

B: Hang on, hang on, all that at once is not normal – surely!

A: Well, do you?

B: ... OK, yes, most of them, but they use so little energy ... It's just easier ...

A: All that energy wasted and you are complaining about a new wind farm which will produce more energy to meet the needs of more and more energy-hungry people.

B: Yes, but I'm not ... Everyone uses ...

A: How about accepting the wind farm as a necessity for our energy production? A necessity brought on by over-consumption. Each time you see it, it could serve as a reminder to use a little less power, as a confession of past energy misuse. You never know, you may come to value it as a harvester of God's natural power!

B: Well, I suppose when you put it like that ... And I could start by turning off a few lights now and then.

Stuart Elliott

GOD IS PRESENT

We believe that God is originator:
dreamer, self-giver, creator, bearer.
WE BELIEVE IN GOD, BEFORE ALL THINGS.

We believe that God is present:
toucher, pain-sharer, life-holder, death-conqueror.
WE BELIEVE IN GOD, FOUND IN ALL THINGS.

We believe that God is mystery:
flowing in deepest darkness, flowing in our waves of fear.
WE BELIEVE IN GOD, DARING ALL THINGS.

We believe that God is waiting:
to bring light, justice, freedom and peace.
WE BELIEVE THAT GOD WILL MAKE ALL THINGS NEW.

John Polhill

SORROW AND HOPE

The earth shudders with each invasion of her perfection:
each species lost;
each spring polluted;
each virgin forest raped.

> Hope dawns with each tree replaced;
> each resource shared;
> each animal protected;
> each right to life respected.

The world shudders with each bomb blast;
each bullet fired;
each revenge plotted;
each life dismissed.

> Hope dawns with each agreement to talk;
> each word of peace;
> each act of reconciliation;
> each life counted as precious.

The Spirit shudders with each closed mind:
each angry word;
each unwilling listener;
each expression of self-satisfaction.

> Hope dawns with increased understanding:
> each hand extended;
> each prejudice overcome;
> each admission of our need for one another.

Julia Morris

RENEW OUR HEARTS

Creator God,
may our hearts of stone
become hearts of flesh
that bleed for all your creation.
Help us to mine deep within
to find courage to continue.
May we use our talents wisely,
use resources justly,
for you have blessed us greatly.

God our Maker, renew our hearts
to work for the good of all creation.

Fiona van Wissen

BROTHER JESUS, STRENGTHEN US

Brother Jesus, come
enter the space
between human desire
and the urging of your Spirit.

You who were tempted
through hunger, come,
enter the space

where a voice urges 'Eat –
eat, for an unknown
farmer ploughs foreign soil
and your own stomach will be full.'

You who were tempted
with all the world's kingdoms, come,
enter the space
where a voice whispers,
'Greed is good,
wealth better
and power best.'

You who fought
system and organisation,
Pharisee and tax collector,
who turned the tables
and reached not towards the arms of angels,
but to the arms of a cross.

Enter our weakness,
strengthen us to challenge,
bless us in the cause of right;
reform us to heaven-shape our world.

Jenny Gregory

THE MUSTARD SEED

Lord –
when I feel paralysed
by the magnitude of the problem ...
    Help me to make a beginning.

When I feel overwhelmed
by facts, figures and issues ...
    Help me to see the way forward.

When I feel despair
at the lack of progress ...

Help me to find fresh hope.

When I feel discouraged
and ready to simply give up ...
Help me to persevere with joy.

When I feel that my small efforts
will not make the slightest difference ...
Help me to remember the mustard seed.

Pat Bennett

LET THIS BE THE DAY

As they face this day, O God,
give bread to those who hunger.
Let this be the day when children's mouths are filled
and swollen bellies are no more.
Let this be the day when bread falls from the sky
and peace reigns on the battlefield.

As they face this day, O God,
give hunger to those who have bread.
Let this be the day that those who have learn to share
and selfishness is smothered by generosity.
Let this be the day when enough is enough
and greed loses its power.

As they face this day, O God,
give bread to those who hunger for a better life.
Let this be the day that fair trade is the only trade
and shops count profits in compassion.
Let this be the day when the empty inside
find your fullness of life.
Let this be the day when the Third World knows justice,
and governments co-operate for good.

Let this be the day ...
but if not today then let it come soon, O God,
when your kingdom comes,

when your love breaks into our world
and we are transformed.

Peter Macdonald

BLESS EACH SMALL ACT

We labour like some paper boat
tossed in a raging sea.
It feels as if the powers that rule our world
will sweep over all our efforts to care, protect, sustain.

And yet we recall the monks of old
who set out in boats of stick and skin
to take your message across their world,
their greatest and their lightest load, your blessing.

So Creator of all that stretches out beyond the dimmest star,
bless each small act, which barely fills a moment of our day,
and join it with a myriad of other deeds,
making a sail to catch your Spirit's breath.

John Polhill

WE JOURNEY ON

Refreshed by the touch of the Creator,
WE JOURNEY ON SINGING GOD'S PRAISE.

Redeemed by the love of Christ,
WE JOURNEY ON SINGING GOD'S PRAISE.

Renewed by the dance of the Spirit,
WE JOURNEY ON SINGING GOD'S PRAISE.

Chris Polhill

HYMN FOR THE GREEN CHURCH

1 Green was the earth when You dreamed it and made it,
2 Gold was the hope when we shared in Your mak - ing,
3 Red is Your pro - mise of jus - tice and heal - ing,

Moun - tains so high, and the wa - ters be - low;
Learned what could grow from the trea - sures we find,
Cost - ing You all, for our sakes, for all life;

Crea - tures so va - ried, of fur, fin and fea - ther
Mined from the ground, from the wa - ter and for - est,
O - pen our hearts to Your grace, now re - veal - ing

Find - ing their home in the sun, wind or snow.
Honed in the test - tube, the cir - cuit, the mind;
New ways to work and move, dream, share and thrive.

Words & melody: © Anna Briggs. Arrangement: © Stephen Alliss.

Made man and wo - man to show forth Your plea - sure,
End - less our hun - ger for great - er pos - ses - sions,
Let us re - joice in Your co - ve - nant rain - bow,

Pro - mised their shel - ter, their free - dom, their food;
Reck - less our use of each fi - nite re - source;
Trust as we trust - ed You through the Great Flood;

Charged them to che - rish Your earth and its trea - sure,
Grey now the skies as we live our ob - ses - sions,
Praise Your a - bun - dance, for - give - ness and wis - dom,

Lit night and day, then You saw it was good.
Wast - ing Your gifts, and with lit - tle re - morse.
Che - rish Your gifts, for we know they are good.

Green was the earth when You dreamed it and made it,
mountains so high, and the waters below;
creatures so varied, of fur, fin and feather
finding their home in the sun, wind or snow.
Made man and woman to show forth Your pleasure,
promised their shelter, their freedom, their food;
charged them to cherish Your earth and its treasure,
lit night and day, then You saw it was good.

Gold was the hope when we shared in Your making,
learned what could grow from the treasures we find,
mined from the ground, from the water and forest,
honed in the test tube, the circuit, the mind;
endless our hunger for greater possessions,
reckless our use of each finite resource;
grey now the skies as we live our obsessions,
wasting Your gifts, and with little remorse.

Red is Your promise of justice and healing,
costing You all, for our sakes, for all life;
open our hearts to Your grace, now revealing
new ways to work and move, dream, share and thrive.
Let us rejoice in Your covenant rainbow,
trust as we trusted You through the Great Flood.
Praise Your abundance, forgiveness and wisdom,
cherish Your gifts, for we know they are good.

Words and melody: Anna Briggs
Arrangement: Stephen Alliss

'Hymn for the Green Church' was one of the winners of the BBC Hymnwriting Competition, 2006

CONTEMPLATE CHRIST'S SACRIFICE
Tune: Proper Sarum melody/ 'Before the ending of the day' (8888)

Before your passion, Jesus Christ,
we contemplate your sacrifice;
that staying true to God's own way,
you give your all, true love display.

While leaders played their power game
your silence put them all to shame.
You taught of costly peace and love,
then showed us on the cross above.

In all life's struggles guide our way,
our choice reflect your love each day.
If facing darkness be our path
help us embrace the cross at last.

For you're beside us, ev'ryone,
the weak or whole, confused or sure.
There is no place you are not found,
your presence makes it holy ground.

Chris Polhill

TRANSFORMATION

METANOIA

'Why do you look for the living among the dead?' (Luke 24:5)

It was on a bright, sunny, stiflingly hot day one week after Easter 1994 that we drove out from the centre of Manila. I was glad of the air conditioning in the van and still reeling from a visit to Smokey Mountain the previous day. Father Ben Beltrane had introduced me there to some of the thousands of people who eked out a living making a few cents daily from scouring through the rubbish on the 200-foot-high smouldering heap from which the place took its name. Ben, a Catholic Priest and academic with a razor-sharp mind and charismatic gifts of leadership, was a man who could command big money from taking up one of the many offers he had received from US colleges over the years. Instead he chose life on the hill, living in community with the poorest of the poor, running a project with slum-dwellers repairing and painting the jeepniks, which are the main mode of transport around Manila.

Not content with survival, however, Ben's whole way of living spoke of transformation: of the physical conditions of the poor; of the lives of the ravaged and abandoned; of the spirits of the downcast and downtrodden. As a community organiser, Ben has few equals. He puts his intellectual and political skills to taking on the government – not alone, but in partnership with those most affected, the dwellers of Smokey Mountain. As he put it himself:

> *'You have to have a dream, and believe that it's not your destiny, that it's not God's will for you to be impoverished like that. We marched on the street and forced the government to rehabilitate the dump. That got us to where we are now.'*

And where are 'we' now? The dump was officially shut down in 1995 and new blocks of social housing began to appear, funded by a coalition of partners, including the government. More than 20,000 former slum-dwellers live in these basic but adequately resourced homes, a far cry from the old shanties of the Mountain. The benefits are not only for those folks; the removal of a huge source of pollution and disease brings renewal and transformation for all around. It may only be a drop in the ocean of what is needed in terms of resurrection for the poor of Manila, but it is a start, a tangible sign of hope. Here at least, the living are no longer among the dead.

As we came towards the shoreline, the sun suddenly began to disappear in a haze. At first I thought it was a fog blowing in from the sea, but the acrid smell was all too familiar from the day before. The stench of burning rubbish in the slums of the world is something you can only comprehend if you have breathed it in. After a few minutes we drew to a halt outside a high, white-washed wall. It took a moment in the fog of smoke to realise that we had stopped outside a cemetery.

Stepping from the van, we entered a graveyard. The first impression was that it had been a grand setting some time past. This was a place where the rich had come to rest. A number of the tombs were small houses, with a little courtyard at the front, Grecian pillars opening into a room where a large sarcophagus (or two) looked rather like a kind of macabre table. I was immediately struck by the irony that, even in death, the rich had a far better place to occupy than the living of the shanty towns.

Then came another shocking realisation – something moved in the corner of one of the marbled rooms. Another, and another appeared, emerging like spectres in the blue-grey haze. Hundreds of people were living in this place of death. A whole new ring came to the angel's question: '*Why do you look for the living among the dead?*'

Within seconds, people appeared from every corner of the cemetery, gathering around Ramos, my guide, an aid worker involved in community organising in a number of the slums of Manila. They chattered excitedly together in Spanish and I caught no more than every tenth word. What was self-evidently clear was that they knew and trusted one another. We pressed on towards the back wall of the grave-yard, which was broken down in places. I began to make out the sea in the distance, but in front of it was a 'beach' made up of tons of rubbish, not dissimilar to the mountain we had visited. It was covered with people sifting and gathering, hauling bags of plastic bottles or aluminium cans unearthed with bare hands from the mass of rotting garbage. The scene was a hellish kind of Costa del Sol: a crowded beach of a different magnitude. A filthy black sludge replaced lapping blue water – but children still paddled and swam in it.

Ramos explained the excitement: As squatters in this graveyard, the people were vulnerable not only to the disease that such squalor inevitably brings, but also to the violence of the authorities and the rich landowners. On several occasions, they had been raided at night by thugs with baseball bats and even guns, beating and terrorising them out of the tombs. Each time they were evicted, however, the people gradually drifted back, but always with the same fear of violence and death. On more than one occasion, people had died from injuries sustained in the eviction 'process'. But through a series of peaceful protests, followed ultimately by a round-table meeting, the people had found the courage, with the help of community organisers, to confront the authorities. The cemetery had been unused for many years and it clearly provided shelter for many people who had nowhere else to lay their head. There was no question of the land being used for development and there were no relatives of the long-deceased occupants who wanted to visit the tombs. Agreement had been reached, therefore, that no more evictions would take place – a huge relief to those for whom this was home. It might not yet be the social housing being built elsewhere, but at least this place of the dead could be put to better use as a place of the living!

In time, small businesses would be seeded around the cemetery and along the seafront: home industries using the skills of the people to create crafts, often from recycled goods. The long-term aim would be to transform the place in the same way as Smokey Mountain, not simply through pouring in aid money, but much more through harnessing and enabling the skills of people whose human worth and dignity would at the same time be restored.

It may seem like a small step, but these small green shoots of life are the signs of true transformation. With the Easter story of resurrection from the depths of human violence and suffering still fresh in my ears, these encounters with the poor of Manila brought home the joy of what real transformation is all about. Where dignity is restored and hope engendered, the resurrection life is no longer merely 'a conjuring trick with bones', as theologian David Jenkins once so rightly put it. When the path to justice begins to be opened up for the poor and the discarded, the transforming love of the Risen Christ takes on a tangible presence. As small signs of life poke their incredibly vulnerable heads above the injured soil, the healing of the earth and the wholeness of humanity become a dreamed-of possibility.

'*Why do you look for the living among the dead?*' – because that's where transformation is taking place. By definition, resurrection can only come when death and suffering are experienced. They leave their mark upon us, in the same way that the Risen Christ bears the marks of crucifixion. We must not imagine that resurrection masks fear or disguises death. Rather, it is in the very midst of death that the transformed life takes hold and hope springs eternal.

Christ has risen and forever
Lives to challenge and to change
All whose lives are messed or mangled,
All who find religion strange.
Christ is risen, Christ is present
Making us what he has been –
Evidence of transformation
In which God is known and seen.

From 'Christ has risen', by John L. Bell and Graham Maule

Martin Scott

TRANSFORMATION:
LITURGICAL RESOURCES

GOD'S POWER TO SAVE

Transforming God, we come to worship you:
TO JOIN YOUR RESURRECTION DANCE.

With all our struggles and failures,
YOUR POWER ALONE WILL SAVE US.

When the darkness overwhelms us,
YOUR POWER ALONE WILL SAVE US.

When death faces us,
YOUR POWER ALONE WILL SAVE US.

So we praise you, the God who transforms us.
THREE-IN-ONE GOD DANCING BESIDE US.

Chris Polhill

WE OPEN OURSELVES TO GOD

Eternal God, we open our hearts to you:
BREATHE ON WHAT IS HARDENED, THAT WE MAY LOVE AGAIN.

Incarnate Christ, we open our minds to you:
TOUCH WHAT IS BLINDED, THAT WE MAY SEE ALL LIFE ANEW.

Transforming Spirit, we open our wills to you:
FREE WHAT IS BOUND, THAT WE MAY MOVE UPWARDS AND OUTWARDS.

Living Trinity:
WE OPEN OURSELVES TO YOU.
COME IN, WE PRAY, THAT WE MAY LIVE.

Pat Bennett

OPEN OUR HEARTS TO LOVE

Christ, in whom we live and move and have our being,
forgive us who hammer the nails ever harder
into the green wood of your creation.
Open our eyes to see you in all things,
open our hearts to your love for all your works,
open our minds to your wisdom and humility,
that we might take our rightful place in your world,
loving what you love,
and longing for the day when all creation
will be transfigured through your resurrection life.

Simon Davis

HELD IN RELATIONSHIP

Creator God,
your love calls forth beetles and butterflies.
You speak in tendrils of green growth
and the stark beauty of scree slopes.

Help us to see ourselves as precious and vulnerable,
held in relationship with all creation
by the Divine breath of love.
Amen

Caroline Leys

BIN-DAY CONFESSION

You might need to alter the colours and bins/boxes/bags as local collections determine.

On 'brown bin day', I offer these things not as rubbish to be thrown away, but with the hope that the potential within them can be released into life-giving, nutritious compost:

grass cuttings,
pruned twigs from hedges,
dead flower heads,
failed vegetables ...

I offer them as a confession of my need for perfect lawns, neatly trimmed hedges and tidy flowerbeds.

As I give them up let them be a reminder to be less concerned about the edges of the lawn and the shape of the hedges, even to enjoy the shape and colour of weeds.

On 'blue box day', I offer these things not as rubbish, but with the hope that they have the potential to be recycled into something new by those who need these precious resources:

plastic milk bottles,
glass jars,
food packaging,
tin cans ...

I offer them as a confession of my hunger for processed foods, convenience meals, exotic treats preserved and shipped from all corners of this world.

As I give up these things let them be a reminder to shop locally, eat seasonally and buy unprocessed foods.

On 'blue bag day', I offer all the paper that has come into the house:

half-read newspapers,
junk mail,
envelopes,
shredded bills and bank letters,
catalogues full of stuff we can live without and ill afford ...

I offer these with the hope that they can be created into new paper – new words and offers that may inspire, teach and re-create.

As I give these up I remember the hours of work that have gone into the writing, editing, printing and publishing, all giving employment.

On 'black bag day', I give up my share of what we all cannot deal with.

As I fill this bag with all the unwanted things that cannot be recycled I am joined to others, linked with those who take away our rubbish and hide it from our eyes. I add to this bag worries and hurts caused to others, the unseen consequences of past actions, pledging to put out a slimmer bag next week.

Stuart Elliott

TEACH US TO TRUST

We confess that we despair too easily,
become frozen in fear at the environmental nightmare,
angry in our denials that something is wrong,
protective of resources that we need to share,
blind to the need for fundamental change,
deaf to the consequences for the poor.

Forgive our fear and our anger.
Teach us to risk gospel-style sharing,
to see where change can begin,
to respond to the cries of the poor.
Increase our faith in your renewing love
that we may see heaven on earth.

Chris Polhill

A VERSION OF PSALM 19

All: THE UNIVERSE, VAST BEYOND OUR IMAGINING, SPEAKS OF GOD'S GLORY.
         THE EARTH, CRADLING THE SMALLEST FLOWER, TELLS US GOD IS NEAR.

A: Time spins out your story;
         its thread runs through our lives.

B: No billboard carries its message,
         no soundbite captures your Word.

A: And yet the narrative is all around us,
         everything has its origin in you.

B: Earth – like a grain of sand
         on the beach of the universe –

A: holds, for a flickering moment of its life,
         the human frame.

B: Sun, water, air and land combine
         for a moment's cradling of our ways.

A: When we follow the patterning of your creation
         and hallow the gifts that surround us,

B: then we know true happiness
         and are able to make wise choices for our lives.

A: Your message is plain for us to see,
         inspiring and energising us.

B: When we co-operate with creation
         it showers gifts upon us.

A: Gifts that outlast human wealth,
         food that satisfies completely.

B: As we begin to live gently,
         so gentleness surrounds us.

A: But sometimes it's hard to know what's right:
         protect us from pride and self-deception.

B: Help us to recognise selfish actions,
      so that they do not become
      the foundation of our lives.

ALL: MAY WHAT WE THINK AND SAY ALWAYS
      BE WOVEN IN THE FABRIC OF YOUR WAY.

John Polhill

A MEDITATION ON THE LORD'S PRAYER

A: Our father
B: who formed the cosmos, knit us in the womb *(Gen 1, Ps 139:13)*

A: in heaven
B: seated on a throne, beneath the seraphim *(Is 6:1)*

A: hallowed be your name
B: let everything that has breath praise the Lord *(Ps 150:6)*

A: Your kingdom come
B: creation waits in eager expectation *(Rom 8:19)*

A: Your will be done
B: they will beat their swords into ploughshares *(Mic 4:3)*

A: on earth as it is in heaven
B: the wolf will live with the lamb *(Is 11:6)*

A: Give us this day our daily bread
B: fruit of the earth and the work of human hands

A: And forgive us our sins
B: when there is no rain because your people have sinned *(1 Kings 8:35)*

A: as we forgive those who sin against us
B: whatever you bind on earth will be bound in heaven *(Mt 18:18)*

A: Do not bring us to the time of trial
B: do not worry *(Mt 6:25)*

A: but deliver us from evil

B: under his wings you will find refuge *(Ps 91:4)*

A: for thine is the kingdom

B: you laid the earth's foundation *(Job 38:4)*

A: the power

B: you give orders to the morning *(Job 38:12)*

A: and the glory

B: you bring forth the constellations in their seasons *(Job 38:32)*

A: for ever and ever.

B: who was, and is, and is to come *(Rev 4:8)*

A and B: Amen

Eleanor Harris

WHAT DO YOU HOPE FOR THE WORLD?

What do you hope for the world?
What are your dreams?
Peace and justice,
food and shelter,
lands and oceans
that are healthy and clean?

What do you hope for your country?
What are your dreams?
Freedom from oppression,
just and generous government,
available work and adequate housing,
allotments and gardens and city parks?

What do you hope for your friends and family?
What are your dreams?
Health and prosperity,
love between each other,
safe spaces to grow up in,
safe places to grow old?

What do you hope for yourself?
What are your dreams?

(a moment to think)

It's good to dream.
God is always dreaming.

And dreams,
with God's help,
can become reality.

Ruth Burgess

AN IMAGE OF THE FUTURE:
An abandoned motorway

The cars have long since gone from this place.

A barren waste-monument to the automobile that once was king.

A healthy breeze drifts along its length carrying with it dust, grime and dirt, ghosts of the heavy traffic that once flowed along this artery.

A dead, decaying place you might think.

But here and there, among the cats' eyes, a small mound of tarmac is raised up, a slight crack at its centre, no more. A blemish on the smooth charcoal-grey surface. And in the midst of all this bareness and waste ground is the glimmer of life. A small gap leading down to the earth below, hoping for a little light and a drop of rain.

In the dark of this crevice a timid green spear points skyward, reaching desperately for the light.

How far has this shoot pushed up from? How long has it taken for this one shoot to emerge from the dead road around it? How many other shoots died on the way to the surface, creating a crack for this one to follow? Years of unfulfilled growth create the weakness for this one solitary shoot to push above ground.

What would it be like to be that one green spear, the shoot that strikes the air, the first in that place to feel the breeze on its slender leaf and to remember that thousands like it never made it to the surface.

First one, but then afterwards many stronger, larger shoots, flowers perhaps, bloom in the wilderness, and a garden is reborn from the earth. Nature takes back what is rightly hers, swallowing the grey with green.

Stuart Elliott

KOTUKU PENINSULA

I live on an island off the eastern coast of New Zealand. We do not have any mammals naturally inhabiting these islands. Rather, over millennia, the ecological niches were filled by varieties of birds. With the arrival of successive waves of human migration, exotic mammals were introduced. The indigenous bird life has been devastated by predation from some of these mammals – particularly rats. The vegetation has also been affected by browsing mammals.

We are part of a partnership of local landowners who are working together to create a pest-free environment for our New Zealand flora and fauna. We have isolated two hundred and thirty hectares of land by erecting a two-kilometre-length of predator-prevention fencing that stretches from the northern to southern coast across the landwards end of the peninsula. The fence has very fine mesh that prevents mice, rabbits, rats, cats, pigs and livestock from entering the regenerating native forest. Mammals are now being eradicated from the peninsula within the fence perimeter.

As this process is completed, it will be possible to reintroduce varieties of birds that are no longer seen in the area. This peninsula will then become a native nature reserve, with some human households living permanently within the perimeter fence.

Already we are seeing signs of the success of the work undertaken over the past eight years. Small birds are filling the once silent forest with their chatter and song. Large birds are now breeding within the area, and visiting to harvest berries and nectar from the flourishing shrubs and trees. Seedlings are appearing on the forest floor, as seeds have a chance to put down roots and produce shoots undisturbed.

The inexorable tide of creative energy is rising again from the good earth. It is as if the capacity of creation to forgive and renew has been released from the colonisation of inappropriate animals.

Caroline Leys

HOPEFUL AND COMMITTED TO THE LONG HAUL:
Eco-practice at St John the Evangelist Church

St John's, on the corner of Princes Street in Edinburgh, has long been committed to a gospel of social action, expressed, for example, in the murals that several times a year offer passers-by a message on issues of peace, justice and development. We gained an Eco-congregation award in 2005 for our leaflet *Earth Be Glad*, linking climate change to the requirements of Christian living, and giving practical advice. We followed the call of the European Christian Environmental Network to incorporate Creationtide in September worship.

The next move was 'Choose Life', a co-ordinated campaign of monthly gas and electricity meter readings, entered on a web programme that produces an instant updated graph of energy use by the member and the whole group. The number of members participating in this is only a fraction of the church membership though; we still find it hard persuading people that it is an easy motivator for trying ways to reduce our carbon footprints. We are also monitoring energy use in the church and exploring long-term development of renewable energy sources.

A 'Green Ginger Group' works to ensure that carbon reduction is considered in every aspect of church life. We have friendly contacts with similar groups at the three neighbouring Church of Scotland churches with whom we have strong links, and are active in the Edinburgh Network of Eco-congregations. We took part in organising the major Edinburgh Churches' Climate Change Conference in October 2008 (www.edinburghclimate.net).

Our local MPs and MSPs, and some councillors, are committed to combating climate change and are always open to contacts. We join in campaigns for strong climate change bills in Scotland and the UK, and action in the European Union. The scale and urgency of the task is daunting but we are hopeful and committed to the long haul.

www.stjohns-edinburgh.org.uk

Jill Duffield

ENCOURAGING GREENER CHURCHYARDS

The churchyard at St Peter's Holton is managed sensitively and follows a plan produced by Suffolk Wildlife Trust. Monthly churchyard work parties take place that involve people in the village.

St Peter's Spexhall had a free moth survey done in the summer which revealed that 150 species of moths live in the area of the churchyard, including six rare species, one of which is called the Muslin Footman (*Nudaria mundana*). Members of the church are working to minimise the tree pruning during the bird-breeding season, ensuring that there is a range of flowering plants, and keeping the dew pond wet. Additionally, the water used for the graveyard comes from rainwater from the water butt, not mains water from a tap.

Jacqueline Moulson, Church Warden, St Peter's Holton

TRANSFORMING A CHURCHYARD WITH AND FOR ITS LOCAL COMMUNITY

The land for the St Mary & St John churchyard in East Oxford was bought in the 1860s and planted with trees and shrubs to provide an attractive peaceful place where loved ones could be remembered. Unfortunately, 130 years later it had become a derelict, massively overgrown no-go area. In 2000, on the initiative of a community policeman, soldiers cut back the jungle, revealing the many, often dislodged and damaged memorials.

After consulting widely, and with the churchyard closed for burials, the church began managing it for wildlife, with the aim of re-creating a quiet green space for all to enjoy. Old paths were resurfaced, entrances reopened, lighting installed, and a 5-year management plan commissioned to guide the clearing and planting. This required more consultation with experts and residents in the area, more fundraising, and the recruitment of volunteers.

Eight years on, there is a wildflower Garden of Remembrance and Thanksgiving; a mini-labyrinth; a variety of habitats for wildlife; and access to memorials that have artistic and historic value. On-site interpretation boards introduce visitors to both the wildlife and the local history, and there is an educational website: www.ssmjchurchyard.org.uk. Early on, the church registered as an eco-congregation so that the work would be seen as celebrating and caring for God's creation. It is a great outreach project, involving people of different backgrounds and experience, and appreciated by many who have no connection to the church. The gratitude of people who are now able to revisit their family graves has also been very moving.

Ruth Conway

THE KNIGHTSRIDGE BREATHING SPACE PROJECT

It's a very simple story: find a bit of ground in need of some TLC, conjure up some bright ideas for improving the area, fill in endless grant application forms, cheerfully accept rejection from BBC's Breathing Places, chat to your local councillor about your financial problems and – 'Yes, there is a God' – the cheques arrive and the hard work begins.

So what have we been doing for the past two years? We've been organising various community event days to create the 'Knightsridge Breathing Space – A Place of Love, a Place of Peace and a Place of Joy'.

It's been backbreaking digging to prepare the ground for the flowerbeds. It's been lifting slabs, mixing cement and relaying slabs to make sure the garden area is accessible for everyone. It's been repairing and painting fences, painting doors, painting window boxes, painting gates and whitewashing walls.

But we've had a laugh and sat round the table, sharing lots of well-earned bowls of soup and bread.

It's been designing and then painstakingly cutting out and recycling scraps of coloured PVC to create our fantastic Mediterranean murals. It's been hours and hours of cutting and gluing hundreds of small glass tiles to create a magnificent mosaic table.

And through it all we've been in touch with and getting to know men, women and children who are not members of our church and, at the same time, deepening our fellowship with those who are.

It's been cold hands and feet working outdoors recycling wine bottles, mirror, slate and floor tiles to create a mosaic tree. But also sitting cosy in the high school pottery department, creating our flock of ceramic doves. It's been meeting up to discuss the various planting possibilities, and trips to the garden centre. It's been organising the planting of donated shrubs, the bulbs and the hedging, and now, of course, the maintenance of it all.

So now, as the story goes ... we enjoy the fruits of our labour. We sit back and gaze with wonder and amazement at what we have achieved as a community for our community.

Marjory McGhie

THE COACH HOUSE TRUST

My garden opens out onto the lane where the Coach House Trust began, and there is a whole community life that takes place in the lane – one of the reasons I love my garden with no back wall and always go out the back door. I have lived here since 1991 and have seen the whole thing grow and develop. In 1996 someone working for the Richmond Fellowship began gardening with some of his clients in the lane. The sites were where buildings had been demolished and had become a dumping ground for rubbish, infected with vermin and an eyesore for local residents. The Belmont Lane Community Gardens Association was formed to address the issue. Now there are beautiful gardens, made by people coming out of long-term institutional care with a range of mental health, addiction and learning problems.

In 1998, when the opportunity to purchase the old coach houses in Belmont Lane arose, the potential for developing and expanding the work already started was recognised. These buildings had been used by a local tradesman, and, although in need of extensive repair and refurbishment, offered the chance for the project to have its own workshops, office and training space. The Coach House Trust was set up as a limited company with charitable status, and lottery funding helped with the conversion costs.

Local residents can use (and get a key for) the Triangle flower garden and buy veg from the market garden, and there are always things happening. They recycle everything we can take: kitchen waste for their compost bins, garden waste, glass, etc. They have a big garden party in the summer. It's a great sign of what can happen in the middle of the city, just in ground that was neglected and unused, and gives creative and meaningful engagement for people who otherwise have nowhere to belong.

www.thecht.co.uk

Kathy Galloway

ECO-FEST

St John's Church, Neville's Cross, Durham is a church not 'at a crossroads' but *on* a crossroads and as such sees its role as being a centre for a community growing in all directions. In October 2008, St John's held its first Eco-fest.

At the back of the church is a large field and scout hut – an ideal venue for such an event. So, with great faith in the English weather, it was decided to hold an outdoor event, which would be more welcoming to non-churchgoers. The idea was to attract people to the event itself rather than to hold a churchy event, although coincidentally it was held the day before 'Back to Church Sunday'.

The organisers had no idea who might be interested in having a stall at such an event, but after the first few contacts with local organisations – recycling, car-sharing, a greenwood furniture maker – the word soon spread as to what we were planning. 'Yes, I would love to come, but have you asked …?' 'Oh, have you heard of such and such, and so and so?' It was amazing – in a parish where there are only a handful of shops, one pub and two businesses but lots of homes – how many organisations, all related to reducing our carbon footprint and spreading the ethos of sustainability, were interested in coming to our event!

On the day itself some forty organisations were represented. There was a children's area for storytelling, coconut shies, a swap-shop for toys. A hog roast and soup stall satisfied the hunger, and cream teas and coffee indulged the thirsty. A fair trade stall had a constant stream of purchasers and the local organic veg box supplier signed up many new clients. Along with the Mayor, local MP and other councillors, over 500 members of the local community turned up, and that made it all worthwhile. Next year's event is already being planned.

Paul Jefferson

Update: Eco-fest has now become an event that the community is supporting in growing numbers – the 2010 Eco-fest attracted many new organisations, speakers and musicians. A finale of beer and praise proved to be a real show-stopper and will become a permanent fixture.

SWAP RATHER THAN THROW AWAY

We have a Swap day each year now at church. These are occasions when anyone can bring unwanted, good quality household goods and deposit them in the church hall. And anyone can come and take away anything they can use. Most people do both. Completely free!

A grant pays for publicity (including leaflets to deliver to around 2000 local homes) and a van and driver, who picks up large items on the day, brings them to the church, and later delivers them to homes. The aims of the Swap are to keep good quality goods out of the landfill, and to do a good service to the community. It is espe-cially valuable in Eastham, because we have no charity shops and a community of very mixed incomes. The events are very popular with the local community, and we also arrange to have information on energy and water efficiency, recycling, fair trade, etc available. We run swaps with a local charity, Wirral Environmental Network, who started such events a few years ago. They have a system of esti-mating the weight of goods, from which we can say that, on the most recent swap, we re-homed some 2148 kgs, passed 570 kg of saleable goods to various charities, recycled 11 kg, and just 22 kg went to landfill.

Problems? Well, it takes a bit of explaining to the grant-giving bodies just what a swap day is, but once they have the idea, funding has been forthcoming. And there are inevitably some goods left at the end of the day, so a system of contacts is needed: charities who can use or sell, Freecycle members … Oh, and it takes lots of hands to help on the day – and a constant supply of (fair trade) tea!

Hilary Ash, for St David's URC, Eastham, Wirral

ISLAND CASTAWAYS

Getting rid of rubbish, or anything no longer wanted, is a big problem on a small island, like Iona. Or even on a big island – like Mull – with a small population and few facilities for recycling. That was the situation until an enthusiast called Terry Hegerty persuaded the Community Trust to employ him to raise awareness and, in dialogue with Argyll and Bute Council, set up a strategy for recycling. That is how MESS (Mull and Iona Environmentally Sensitive Solutions) began.

Terry rented an office in steadings behind the main street in Bunessan. He had a phone and a computer, and put notices in the shops inviting local folk to come with questions about recycling – with the incentive of a free low-energy light bulb. A few dropped in. He thought more might come if the space was also used for a swap-shop. It began in a small way with a clothes rail, boxes of crockery, baby clothes and CDs. People started donating usable things to 'the MESS shop', rather than putting them in the bin. Others, finding something that they needed, but having nothing to swap, made a donation. Volunteers were recruited to run the shop, and soon it was clear that it was taking off, and making money. This was not the original intention, but after a year several hundred pounds were disbursed to local charities.

By the time Terry moved on, MESS had been instrumental in setting up recycling bins and banks at several points on the islands, with regular collections. Low-priced compost bins had been sold through the project, and many low-energy light bulbs given away. Meanwhile the retail arm of MESS continued to grow. Good quality furniture was being received and sold on. Another shop was opened in Craignure. Bunessan's shop expanded into two more units in the steadings. All items donated are now weighed, so that the Council can keep tally of how much has been diverted from landfill. A shop manager oversees the operation, working with several volunteers.

If you visit the shop in Bunessan – now open six days a week for most of the year – you'll probably be welcomed by Effie Cruden, who keeps it in apple-pie order. She enjoys it when a dining table comes in, so that she can set it with matching china, on a well-ironed cloth, with colour-coordinated vase and candlesticks. Of course, things well displayed sell fast, and she has to begin all over again. As you can imagine, the shop itself, like the imaginative recycling it represents, is anything but a 'mess'. The two shops on Mull are now called, appropriately, Island Castaways.

Jan Sutch Pickard

THE END OF NIGHTMARES ABOUT WATER IN KAMRANG, NEPAL

'Eleven years ago water was extremely scarce in this village and clean drinking water was not available. I had to get up at three o'clock in the morning to collect water. It used to take me more than three hours walking down steep, narrow paths to collect 20 litres of water. Sometimes I even took my children with me to collect a small jar of water.'

These are the words of Mrs Shaili Tithung who has lived in Kamrang, in the hills of Nepal, since she was married 25 years ago. Until 1992 this was her daily ritual which she undertook to collect her family's water.

'Many times I dropped my *gagri* [a vessel to carry water] while walking in the dark along the narrow paths and it rolled down the terraces ... Many people were injured rushing along these paths in the dark. During the dry season I used to have nightmares about water. All the time I had to worry about meeting my family's needs. In those days, I was unable to work in the farm because I had to concentrate on fetching water.'

But since 1992, life in Shaili's village has changed. With support from WaterAid's main Nepalese partner, Nepal Water for Health (NEWAH) and a local NGO, Mahankal Youth Club, a new water scheme was installed in the village.

Now, rather than walking down steep, narrow paths, the villagers are able to collect clean safe water close to home. Sanitation and hygiene education were included in the project and now all of the houses in the village have their own latrines.

From WaterAid
www.wateraid.org

FLOATING GARDENS IN BANGLADESH

When Tara Begum and her family watched floodwater swamp their precious farm-land, they were distraught. But, with the help of Practical Action, they were able to quite literally rise above what nature had thrown at them. Using a technique Practical Action had already shared with thousands of other families like Tara's, they constructed a garden that simply floated several feet above where Tara had once grown crops. What's more, because the garden is made from layers of water hyacinths, bamboo, compost and cow dung, all the necessary materials are easily obtainable and affordable.

Rather than being at the mercy of the floods, it meant Tara could grow red onions, *kang kong* (a leafy vegetable), okra and saplings for sweet pumpkin – as well as seedlings for gourds, which she was able to transplant when the floods died down. In Tara's words: 'Before I had no means to feed my children. Now I even have enough to sell at market – and my neighbours have copied the gardens so they can do the same.'

From Practical Action
www.practicalaction.org

RAINWATER HARVESTING IN INDIA

Water harvesting resurrects the *tanka* method of irrigation that was common across India until the early nineteenth century, and involves collecting the monsoon rain in specially dug ponds. Rather than evaporate or flow away in flash floods, the water is able to percolate down through the soil to revitalise the water table and, in turn, refill village wells.

Retired police officer Haradevsingh Hadeja's development of the drainage system in his village of Rajsamadhiya proved so successful that for over a decade the community has not needed the service of the government water tankers on which other local villages depend for drinking water. It also means that newly irrigated crops are flourishing, and ponds and wells are full. Once the water table was 30m (98ft) down; today it is only 7m (23ft) down.

Fred Pearce, from *New Scientist*, February 2006
www.newscientist.com/article/mg18925401.500

WANGARI MAATHAI AND THE GREEN BELT MOVEMENT

In 2004 Wangari Maathai was awarded a Nobel Peace Prize Laureate in international recognition for her inspirational work across Kenya. In 1977 she founded the Green Belt Movement, a tree-planting campaign, in a bid to reforest her homeland and create employment. Once regarded as a dissident, she was eventually made Kenya's Assistant Minister for the Environment because of her valuable work.

It was while she was a professor in the University of Nairobi's Faculty of Veterinary Medicine in the 1970s, visiting rural areas, that she first began to make the connections between local people's unfulfilled basic needs such as firewood, clean water and nutritious food, and the conversion of Kenya's indigenous forests into plantations for cash crops. She noted that without adequate vegetation knitting it together, topsoil was being washed away in the rains, leading to widespread land degradation.

Via a National Council of the Women of Kenya forum, Maathai suggested that women engage in tree-planting not only to combat soil erosion but also to provide wood and as a food source. She was thus regarded as rebellious, not for the actual tree-planting, but because its very organisation emphasised the mismanagement of the environment by other interests.

Today Wangari Maathai's work is deeply respected in her homeland and across the world … In the rural communities of the developing world, women's voices and experiences are often disregarded in spite of their rich and vital contribution to society. Maathai's tree-planting initiative is a parable in itself: out of little seedlings, women have gained confidence in what they have to offer and how they can change the world for good.

Catherine von Ruhland,
from *Living with the Planet: Making a Difference in a Time of Climate Change*

AN INDIAN ROPE TRICK

A Rocha India has transformed the conflict of interests between elephants and farmers in India. The breakthrough has come by adapting a method trialed in Africa and targeting the elephants' most highly developed sense – smell. A concoction of oil, ground chilli and tobacco is smeared on ropes which are strung round the perimeter of crop fields. Elephants dislike the pungent smell, which creates a barrier that is psychological, physical and very effective. From initial scepticism, local villagers have been won over and are now enthusiastic.

A 90-day trial involving 8 villages has been overwhelmingly successful … The success story has now reached the national press, and forest officials from as far away as Sri Lanka have been to visit to learn from A Rocha's work.

From an A Rocha newsletter

A Rocha is a Christian nature conservation organisation, our name coming from the Portuguese for 'the Rock', as the first initiative was a field study centre in Portugal. A Rocha projects are frequently cross-cultural in character, and share a community emphasis, with a focus on science and research, practical conservation and environmental education. (From the A Rocha website: www.arocha.org)

WE BELIEVE

A: We believe in God the Creator,
       who reminds us, in the dawning rays of every new day,
       that new life is possible.
       We believe in the wonder and grandeur of a universe
       where the whole of life is called to live
       in a harmony of care.

ALL: THIS WE BELIEVE.

B: We believe in Jesus Christ,
       who prayed in mountains of peace,
       and brought us the Word
       in mustard seeds of faith and fig trees of blessing,
       whose footsteps touched the earth in love
       and who invites us to follow.

ALL: THIS WE BELIEVE.

A: We believe in the Holy Spirit,
       whose wisdom often lies
       embedded in ancient peoples.
       They trod lightly across deserts and
       lived gently among plants and creatures.
       They reached respectfully for the mystery,
       which is God-with-us,
       the One who never leaves us nor forsakes us.

ALL: THIS WE BELIEVE.

B: We believe in everlasting hope,
       the great calling of the people of God, the church,
       for the transforming of all things,
       which is possible in God.

ALL: THIS WE BELIEVE. AMEN

Dorothy McRae-McMahon, Uniting Church in Australia

LEAVES

Leaves
remind us
there is a time
to let go:

let go gently
and flutter to the ground
or be forced to let go in a violent storm.

When they are gone – every last one –
the promise held in each bare branch
is that one day they will return
and grow,
and blaze with colour again.

Fiona van Wissen

THE CIRCLE

I stand within my circle,
that sacred space within,
where I feel secure
where the real me stands tall
and all my tasks and barriers lie broken at my feet.

I stand – my face turned to the sun,
my arms upstretched,
embracing life's joys –
a windswept mountain,
a heartfelt touch,
a centredness of being.

I stand beneath life's darkness
within the fires of my pain –
a wounded soul ...
... open to life's painful cleansing,
my face turned to the stars.

I stand amidst the turmoil of life,
its swirling currents
and ever-changing faces.
Allowing its winds to rush through me.
Touching me. Changing me.

Different, yet the same
I stand
within that sacred space.

Rowena Aberdeen

SIGNS

Spring:
the resurrection life of tiny things –
a baby's head, unfurling leaves,
emerging insect wings,
astounding, new,
immaculately velvet, touched with dew,
uncoiled from dark confinement,
blindly breaking through,
reaching for light and life.

Though winter's desolation, nights of rain,
persuade that dawn will never break
or blood be warm again,
the first signs show:
as sturdy shoots press up beneath the snow,
reliable as sunrise,
then by faith we know
there will be light and life.

Spring:
All health and hope hang trembling by a thread
and we must perish, take our place
with long-forgotten dead,
return to dust.

But we have seen the spring, and learned to trust
the signs of resurrection,
that we surely must
waken to light and life.

Marnie Barrell

FIT US TO BE EASTER PEOPLE

Jesus Christ,
tempted to turn stones to bread
in the wilderness:
teach us that when we change time
for our convenience –
     night to day in our living;
     patience to speed in our journeying;
     winter to summer in our eating –
we change God's calendar which brings
     the hatchling to the caterpillar;
     the bee to the nectar;
     the rains to the farmer;
to the one which brings you to the cross.

Give us grace in our simplest actions
to choose the life which breathes
in the beautiful complexity of creation,
to conquer death,
and to fit us to be Easter people. Amen

Eleanor Harris

RESURRECTION HOMES

Jesus Christ,
in changing weather, vanishing species
and impoverished neighbours,
the heavens and the earth bear witness against us.
As you lit an Easter fire and cooked breakfast,
fashioning God's kingdom
from the stuff of this earth,
so when we cook and light and warm our homes
make us people of your resurrection,
choosing life
through simplicity, ingenuity and obedience.
Amen

Eleanor Harris

REFINE US IN YOUR FIRE

Let us pray for the transformation of ourselves, and of God's world.
LORD, REFINE US IN YOUR FIRE.

That, as you led your son through death,
you might roll back the stone of little faith.
LORD, REFINE US IN YOUR FIRE.

That we may see anew the earth that is ours,
and dream anew of an earth that is yours.
LORD, REFINE US IN YOUR FIRE.

That, as you walked in your garden in the evening,
our steps may be light on its paths.
LORD, REFINE US IN YOUR FIRE.

That, as you invited all to your table,
earth's stores may be open to all people.
LORD, REFINE US IN YOUR FIRE.

That wolf and hare, lion and lamb,
people in conflict, may lie down together.
LORD, REFINE US IN YOUR FIRE.

That, as no pain of the earth is denied you,
so nothing is denied your resurrection life.
LORD, REFINE US IN YOUR FIRE.

That, as your hands brought us to birth,
ours may be midwives of your new creation.
LORD, REFINE US IN YOUR FIRE.

That, as you looked on your work and called it good,
you may look upon ours, and call it blessed.
LORD, REFINE US IN YOUR FIRE.

Jenny Gregory

TREAD THE EARTH LIGHTLY

We will tread the earth lightly
SCATTERING GOD'S BLESSING.

Our hearts changed by love:
THE LOVE OF THE LIVING GOD.

Working to transform the world –
INSPIRED BY THE HOLY GOD.

Chris Polhill

MAY WE DISPLAY YOUR LIKENESS

God of transforming power,
because we have encountered you –
WE CAN NO LONGER BE AS WE ONCE WERE.

And so, from this moment onwards,
MAY WE DARE TO FOLLOW YOU TO NEW PLACES.

In our looking and seeing,
MAY WE DISCOVER YOUR IMPRINT THROUGHOUT THE WORLD.

Amongst our listening and hearing,
MAY WE DISCERN YOUR VOICE CALLING US TO CHANGE.

Through our speaking and sharing,
MAY WE DISCLOSE THE LANGUAGE AND ACTIONS OF LOVE.

By our living and doing,
MAY WE DECLARE YOUR CARE FOR ALL OF CREATION.

And, as we are thus transformed by you,
SO MAY WE DISPLAY YOUR LIKENESS.

Pat Bennett

TRANSFORM OUR LIVES

May God who established the dance of creation,
who marvelled at the lilies of the field,
who transforms chaos to order,
lead us to transform our lives and the Church
to reflect God's glory in creation.

From Eco-congregation

GOD, IN YOUR GRACE

Tune: Per Harling

(♩ = 110)

1 Love is your way, love is your na - ture, bless - ing each
2 Path - ways we choose, un - de - served free - dom, earth as our
3 Ter - ror and tears, wounds with - out heal - ing, hearts with - out
4 Let us stand still, look at each o - ther, sis - ter and

crea - ture, light - ing each day; grace is your sign,
king - dom, still we a - buse; much we have done,
feel - ing mir - ror our fears: life with - out trust,
bro - ther thwart - ing your will: teach us good care,

gift of for - give - ness, cha - lice that chan - ges wa - ter to wine.
gross hu - man er - ror, mis - use of pow - er dark - ens the sun.
greed and high pri - ces, con - flict and cri - sis grind us to dust.
grace to seek par - don, re - claim your gar - den, rich - es to share.

God, in your grace, God in your mer - cy, turn us to you to trans-

-form the world, turn us to you to trans - form the world!

Words: Shirley Erena Murray, Music: Per Harling © 2005 Hope Publishing Company, Carol
Stream, IL 60188. All rights reserved. Used by permission

Refrain: *God, in your grace,*
God in your mercy,
turn us to you
to transform the world!

Love is your way,
love is your nature,
blessing each creature,
lighting each day;
    grace is your sign,
    gift of forgiveness,
    chalice that changes
    water to wine –
God, in your grace …

Pathways we choose,
undeserved freedom,
earth as our kingdom,
still we abuse;
    much we have done,
    gross human error,
    misuse of power
    darkens the sun –
God, in your grace …

Terror and tears,
wounds without healing,
hearts without feeling
mirror our fears:
    life without trust,
    greed and high prices,
    conflict and crisis
    grind us to dust –
God, in your grace …

Let us stand still,
look at each other,
sister and brother
thwarting your will:
    teach us good care,
    grace to seek pardon,
    reclaim your garden,
    riches to share –
God, in your grace …

Shirley Erena Murray

MAKER OF MYSTERY
Tune: Down Ampney (Come down, O Love Divine)

Maker of mystery,
dreamer of what will be,
wellspring and fertile ground of all our growing:
tending the buried seed,
foreseeing every need,
you draw us into life beyond our knowing.

Christ, strong and living vine
spreading through space and time,
deep-rooted in the love of God our Mother:
dying, you live and share
your strength with us, to bear
ripe fruit in season for the life of others.

Wild Spirit, springing green,
coiled in the depths unseen,
promise of seed within the fruit maturing:
new life, you grow and swell,
burst from the outgrown shell,
hundredfold yield in every age ensuring.

Living and loving God,
sing in the pulse of our blood;
help us to know you in your own creation,
love you, the life of all,
serve you and hear your call
from our first forming to our full salvation.

Marnie Barrell

APPENDIX

A LECTIONARY FOR CREATION TIME

	Year A	Year B	Year C
Week 1	Job 37:14–24 Psalm 130 Revelation 4 Matthew 8:23–27	Isaiah 55:6–13 Psalm 104:1–23 2 Corinthians 9:6–12 Mark 4:1–9	Genesis 1:1–25 Psalm 19 Revelation 3:14–22 John 1:1–5
Week 2	Job 38:1–18 Psalm 139:1–14 Romans 1:18–25 Matthew 5:13–16	Genesis 2:4–7, 15–24 Psalm 104:24–35 1 John 1:1–4 John 2:1–11	Genesis 1:26–2.3 Psalm 8 Colossians 1:15–20 John 1:6–18
Week 3	Deuteronomy 28:1–14 Psalm 65 2 Corinthians 9:6–15 Luke 12:16–30	Deuteronomy 8:7–18 Psalm 126 1 Timothy 6:6–10 Matthew 6:25–33	Deuteronomy 26:1–11 Psalm 100 Philippians 4:4–9 John 6:25–35
Week 4	Leviticus 25:1–7 Psalm 95 Hebrews 4:1–11 John 6:1–15	Ecclesiastes 3:1–8 Psalm 98 Romans 8:14–25 Mark 4:26–32	Proverbs 8:1–4, 22–31 Psalm 148 Acts 17:22–34 Matthew 6:19–24
Week 5	Leviticus 25.8–19 Psalm 33:1–12 1 Timothy 2:1–7 Luke 17:11–19	Isaiah 40:21–31 Psalm 24 Revelation 21:1–7 Luke 7:1–10	Genesis 9:8–17 Psalm 67 1 Corinthians 10:23–31 Matthew 5:43–48

Notes

1. *Creation Time was initiated by some Orthodox churches and is promoted by the European Christian Environment Network. The aim is to bring this major theological theme into the liturgical calendar.*

2. It is recommended that Creation Time be celebrated in September and early October.

3. The readings for the third week of this lectionary are those for Harvest Thanksgiving in the Church of England Common Worship Lectionary. *The readings for the fifth week might be suitable for marking One World Week.*

4. This lectionary was produced for use in the parishes of Pilton, Croscombe, North Wootton and Dinder in the Diocese of Bath and Wells. It is not an authorised lectionary of the Church of England.

David Osborne

LITURGY AND TRANSFORMATION

To be human is to breathe in and out, to act and to reflect. The transformation of the world is the result of action and reflection together. Liturgy is part of that reflection at depth, without which the transformation of human beings and the world is impossible.

Liturgy orders time, patterning the year, usually according to the seasons, and relating them to particularly important events in the life of the community and of the individual members of that community. This function of liturgy is given a particular dynamic by the gospel. Christian liturgy orders time by interpreting time. The year starts four weeks before the birth of the Messiah, in Advent. It is marked from the start, therefore, by judgement and hope, a call to self-criticism, and a promise that something new is possible. The winter solstice is read through John 1:5: 'The light shines in the darkness, and the darkness has not overcome it.' Darkness is read through martyrdom (St Stephen's Day, 26th December) and the Slaughter of the Innocents (28th December) but is followed by Epiphany – the manifestation of glory. Traditionally the spring festival salvaged meaning through the cycle of death and rebirth, but the Christian liturgy proclaims us prisoners of hope (Zech 9:12) reading the whole of creation through the promise of resurrection (Rom 8:18f). Liturgy is transformative, therefore, because it teaches us to read the everyday in terms of what is new and hopeful. Likewise Pentecost, the old Palestinian festival of the first fruits, invites us to see the Wisdom of God active and energising in all creative processes.

Liturgy weaves together past and present, in doing so pointing a way into the future. It takes the words of scripture, and especially of the psalms, and uses them as the warp on which the weft of the present is to be woven. All authentic liturgies reach back through countless translations to the cries, perceptions and intuitions of ancient Israel, of Jesus and the communities which first witnessed to cross and resurrection. Liturgies protest the suggestion that reality amounts to nothing, is a tale told by an idiot, and is going nowhere. They do so by celebrating a Name, the Name of God.

Liturgy exists to interrogate our present with that depth, to reflect on the past and to point to the future. It represents the conviction that humans are deep-water creatures: they may enjoy playing in the shallows for a while but if they stay there too long they shrivel and finally die. Liturgy is the deep waters of two and a half thousand years of human wrestling with the question of meaning, the echo of an answer which we call 'revelation', moments and persons where light seems to pierce the darkness. For Christians the heart of that revelation is the life, death and resurrection of Jesus, and because of that the tradition, without which he cannot be understood, the Hebrew Bible. Liturgy ruminates on that tradition. A product of that rumination is the Christian Name for God, the Trinity. Liturgy reads our present and the whole of reality within the Trinitarian history of God. Because God has a history, liturgy is structured as narrative. The hidden God is witnessed to in narratives of slavery, oppression, liberation, exile, crucifixion and dispersion. The creed, used in many liturgies, is essentially the bullet points of a story, prose poetry reflecting on the significance of the events surrounding Jesus. It offers us the 'meta-narrative' to understand our own stories by, in opposition to the reigning narrative of the market.

The ancient circle dances, which still form part of the Ethiopian Orthodox liturgy, are models of all liturgies. They establish rhythms of speech, memory and footfall. They are ways of learning a language and living within it. People sometimes worry that liturgy is 'mechanical' and that it does not involve the worshippers. But liturgy is a familiar dance in which one slips in and out. It does not call for brow-furrowing attention. Its familiarity is the ground for freedom, surprise and innovation. Liturgy, by its ordered arrangement, helps us to make sense of our world. It establishes habits of the heart, patterns our gait. Habits of the heart, of course, can be reactionary rather than transformative and this means that not just any liturgy will do. Like the church, liturgy is always in the process of being reviewed. The criterion for this is faithfulness to the story.

Good Friday and the Day of Atonement cut vertically across the ordered rhythm of the seasons. Remembered in every liturgy they allow oppressed, which is to say, divided, unauthentic ('sinful') beings to face the fact that they are themselves hosts of the oppressor, and therefore need to take steps towards liberation. Christian liturgy systematically addresses the shadow in human beings on the understanding that transformation can only come through the healing of brokenness. Liturgy is transformative precisely as it is a cry for healing. 'How can we sing the Lord's song in a strange land?'(Ps 137). The strange land is the land of our bondage, marked every single day in a thousand ways in the newspapers. How could we live without lament? Life without it would be intolerably shallow. Good Friday, recalled at every Eucharist, confronts the terror of history, remembering every form of crucifixion. Liturgy puts hope in place of optimism because nothing can be changed if evil is not faced. Reflecting on this Paul wove into his reflections on cross and resurrection the idea of justification. The cross critiques and condemns evil but it does not stop there: it affirms life, it says 'Yes' to human beings and to creation.

The Sabbath, too, is an ordering of time that is not given in the seasons or in natural law. In industrial society it became simply a day to 'recharge our batteries', to prepare better for another week's work, but the Sabbath is not rest from labour but God's completion of creation, festival. For both Judaism and Christianity, therefore, Sabbath or Sunday is a feast day, the anticipation of the renewal of creation. This has implications for our understanding of liturgy. In the first place, we could understand that the high purpose of liturgy is transformation. But this is to get things the wrong way around. The liturgy is essentially feast; it is 'purpose-free rejoicing in God'. As it happens, nothing could be more transformative, but that is not the point. Liturgy is first and foremost an expression of love and praise: it is not functional. We do not do it for anything, and certainly not as psychic escape or spiritual cleansing or renewal, any more than we love someone for these reasons.

Second, this determines the character of our celebrations. If the purpose of our liturgy is primarily the reaffirmation of group identity then the presence of strangers is obtrusive, nor do we wish our solemnity to be disturbed. At the feast, however, strangers are welcome and there is room for surprise. The Roman Catholic Church now introduces the Lord's Prayer with the words: 'We pray for the coming of the Kingdom as Jesus taught us.' Liturgy reminds us of the coming Kingdom, of the new order, of the messianic feast without end. This frees us from resignation on the one hand, and fanaticism on the other: it sets life under the sign of the Triune history and invites us to dance. It transforms us with hope.

Timothy Gorringe

SOURCES AND ACKNOWLEDGEMENTS

'God's light and love' – From Eco-congregation Module 2, 'Celebrating Creation' © Eco-congregation. Used with permission of Eco-congregation www.ecocongregation.org

'Oh the life of the world' – Words © Kathy Galloway, music © Ian Galloway, arrangement © John L. Bell, Church of Scotland Panel on Worship, from *Iona Abbey Music Book: Songs from the Iona Abbey Worship Book*, Wild Goose Publications, 2003.

'Rainbow prayer for Operation Noah' – Used with permission of Operation Noah www.operationnoah.org

'Seeking a new relationship' – From Eco-congregation © Eco-congregation. Used with permission of Eco-congregation www.ecocongregation.org

'Keeping food under wraps' – by Simon Parke, originally published in *Church Times*, 23 May 2008. Used by permission of Simon Parke.

'Prodigal civilisation' – by Chris Sunderland, from EarthAbbey www.earthabbey.com Used with permission of Chris Sunderland.

'Affirmation' – From *Iona Abbey Worship Book*, Wild Goose Publications, 2001 © Iona Community.

Passages from Good News Bible – © 1994 published by the Bible Societies/HarperCollins Publishers Ltd UK, *Good News Bible* © American Bible Society 1966, 1971, 1976, 1992. Used with permission.

Passages from NRSV – Copyright 1989, Division of Christian Education of the National Council of the Churches of Christ in the United States of America. Used by permission. All rights reserved.

Psalm 51 – Scripture quotations from *The Message*, copyright (c) by Eugene H. Peterson 1993, 1994, 1995, 1996, 2000, 2001, 2002. Used by permission of NavPress Publishing Group.

'Kajiado Project story' – From Practical Action. Used by permission of Practical Action. http://practicalaction.org

'In Kenya pastoralist communities ...' from Christian Aid's paper, *Time for Climate Justice 2*, June 2010. Used with permission.

'Weerasinghe's story' – From Practical Action. Used by permission of Practical Action. http://practicalaction.org

'What in the world can be done?' – by Catherine von Ruhland, from *Living with the Planet*

ABOUT THE AUTHORS

Rowena Aberdeen worked on Iona for three years as the MacLeod Centre Warden and now works in school chaplaincy. She has written poetry since early childhood and particularly through her teens and early twenties, the period when 'The Circle' was written.

Judith Allinson, a member of St John's Methodist Church, Settle, North Yorkshire, is a botanist and a teacher. She is web editor for Christian Ecology Link: www.christian-ecology.org.uk

Hilary Ash is a botanist and 'green champion' for St David's URC, Eastham, Wirral, and led the church into the Eco-congregation programme.

Revd Chris Baker is Professor of Environmental Fluid Mechanics at the University of Birmingham, where he is Director of the Birmingham Centre for Railway Research and Education, and an Associate Minister at Christchurch, Lichfield. His research interests include wind effects on buildings, agriculture and people, the aerodynamics of trains, the dispersion of air pollutants, and the effects of climate change on transport systems.

Marnie Barrell teaches piano and secondary school music in Christchurch, New Zealand. She is an Anglican laywoman with a strong interest in theology, liturgy and hymnody, and in her writing she strives for thoughtful contemporary expressions of traditional Christian themes.

Ruth Bell is a recently ordained minister in the Church of Scotland, who is about to leave the seaside and return to the River Clyde, in order to embark upon further study at the University of Glasgow.

Jillian Bray – Artists, musicians and writers make their home on New Zealand's Kapiti Coast. Shirley Erena Murray and Jillian, who live in the area, welcome support for their hymns and choral works in local churches and further afield.

Ruth Burgess now lives in Dunblane, and is enjoying growing vegetables and flowers, walking and using her bus pass.

Sonia Christie is a mum to three children, a professional gardener and writes and campaigns on environmental issues.

Ruth Conway is author of *Choices at the Heart of Technology: a Christian Perspective* (1999, Trinity Press International), leads the Education Group of the European Christian Environmental Network, and shares in the Oxford Diocesan Environment initiatives. She manages the churchyard in her local parish for wildlife.

Joanna, Emily and Sam Crawshaw – 'The hymn 'What the Lord Creates' was written for the Christian Ecology Hymn Competition to the tune of 'Twinkle Twinkle, Little Star', as the tune is a particular family favourite and we wanted to celebrate and thank God for all his creation. It has been sung and enjoyed many times in Burton Leonard Church and we hope you enjoy it too.'

Biddy Crossfield – 'Married to Richard, mum of Annie, Mary and Eve. Homemaker, cake and breadmaker whilst listening to Radio 4! I work with refugees, asylum seekers and Wrexham's roofless people and I love what I do.'

Christine and Michael Davidson attend Abbotsford Parish Church in Clydebank and are both professional scientists. Michael runs an environmental monitoring laboratory, whilst Christine is an academic at the University of Strathclyde.

Simon Davis is an Anglican Priest, Member of the Institution of Engineering and Technology and has an MA in Ecological Theology. Based in rural Staffordshire he keeps chickens and has built a homemade wind generator.

Barry Dickinson – 'Eco-coordinator since 2007 of the award-winning eco-congregations of Nelson Methodist Christ Church/St John Southworth RC Parish; HAPPA environmental volunteer worker since 2007; Methodist Local Preacher since 1961; retired High School Deputy Head teacher and former biology teacher. Been keen on wildlife since a little boy and keen to promote links between Christianity and science.'

Jill Duffield – 'I am a member of St John's and a retired education researcher. I joined the 'Green Ginger Group' in 2005 when we began to work on developing St John's action on climate change.'

Stuart Elliott – Stuart lives in North Wales attempting to re-create community based on sustainable practice. (You can follow his attempt here: www.reluctantordinand.co.uk) He is a member of the Iona Community.

Kathy Galloway is a theologian, writer and activist. A member and former Leader of the Iona Community, she is currently Head of Christian Aid in Scotland.

Tim Gorringe is Professor of Theological Studies at the University of Exeter, and is a priest and smallholder, as well as a member of the Iona Community.

Jenny Gregory is a health visitor and an aspiring children's author. Her spirituality is influenced by her love of nature and the creative arts.

Roddy Hamilton – 'Grew up in Gourock with a view of the hills that changed colour each day. Did part of my training as a minister in Scotland and also rural South Africa. Now live in Clydebank.'

Eleanor Harris has worked and edited worship resources for Eco-Congregation Scotland, European Christian Environmental Network, and Earth be Glad at St John's in Edinburgh, where she gained her love of liturgy as a chorister. These projects, as well as her work on the history of the Edinburgh New Town, and as an illustrator, calligrapher and writer, are collected on her website: www.eleanormharris.co.uk

Jennie Juckes did a degree in agriculture at Wye College. She lives on the Welsh borders. Retired but furious over habitat destruction and loss she has given some acreage over to native indigenous woodland plantation. A lay minister in the parish church she has bene-fited from time as a counsellor with the Church in Wales and as a mission accompanier.

Leanne Langley has worked with children and young people in churches from Texas and North Carolina to Hampshire. A social and music historian by profession, she helped introduce the Workshop Rotation Model of Sunday School at Avenue St Andrew's United Reformed Church, Southampton, in 2003.

Joanna Laynesmith is a medieval historian, mother of two and clergy wife who leads the 6-11s Sunday School and Eco-Congregation 'Green Team' at St John and St Stephen's Church in Reading as well as co-ordinating Reading Christian Ecology Link. She has been a Friend of the Iona Community since 1996. www.greeningstjohns.blogspot.com

Caroline Leys is an Anglican Priest; her major focus is companioning others on their spiri-tual journey. She lives with her husband on an offshore island in New Zealand.

Peter Macdonald is a Church of Scotland minister and currently serves as Leader of the Iona Community.

Marjory McGhie is married to Patrick and has three teenage children, Ingham, Lachlan and Oran. She worships at Knightsridge Church (Livingston Ecumenical Parish) and is a teacher of home economics.

Rev. Dorothy McRae-McMahon is Minister-in-Association with the South Sydney Parish of the Uniting Church in Australia. She is an experienced liturgist who has worked inter-nationally.

Julia Morris – 'A Lay Reader looking forward to retirement; spending more time with three gorgeous grandsons; having the space to paint, write stories and express my 'progressive Christianity' in writing poetry, prayers and liturgies.'

Canon Robin Morrison is the Church and Society Officer for the Church in Wales, con-venes its Environment group and is on the leadership group of the European Christians Environment Network. He has been a hospital, university and industrial chaplain, an assis-tant head of a Community School and a parish priest.

Jacqueline Moulson is a retired Probation Officer who moved to Suffolk four years ago and is now a church warden of a small rural church with an open churchyard, which is managed sustainably in respect of wildlife.

Shirley Erena Murray, born in 1931, is a New Zealander whose words are sung worldwide in Christian response to issues of our time: peace, the environment, racism, inclusiveness, compassion, as well as hymns of praise, the sacraments and ceremonies of the Church, songs for meditation and carols. She has been honoured by her country for services to the community through hymnwriting, and in 2010 was awarded the degree of Hon.D.Litt. by New Zealand's oldest University, of Scots foundation, for her contribution to literature and hymnody.

Bryan Owen writes what he calls 'the poetry of observation' and has published two collections of his work. He regularly tours in the UK and USA performing his work and giving poetry seminars; he lives in Kirkintilloch.

Simon Parke has been both a priest and a supermarket worker, but is now a writer, retreat giver and therapist: www.simonparke.com

Jan Sutch Pickard is a writer and storyteller living on Mull, and a former Warden of the Abbey in Iona.

Chris and John Polhill run the Reflection Gardens, five garden areas on the Christian Spiritual Journey, each with an environmental theme in dialogue with that part of the journey. Their home is heated by wood pellets, and they have a 4-kilowatt photovoltaic cell system. They also have a rain water harvesting system.They both do gardening and offer hospitality. Chris companions people on their spiritual journey and John helps with a gardening project for people with mental health problems. Both Chris and John are members of the Iona Community. www.reflectiongardens.org.uk

Gary Polhill is a scientist and lives in north east Scotland.

Steve Rhodes is a Tutbury resident and is the founder and chair of the Tutbury EcoPower self-sustaining community project. The group has a vision to create a Low Carbon Community over the next ten years, with a hydroelectric scheme powered by the River Dove being the flagship; this will return interest and funds to social investors and to community good causes.

Christopher Rowe – 'I was born in Glasgow, grew up in London, and returned to Scotland in 2000, to work for 3 years at Braendam Family House, a place of respite for those living in poverty. I am married to Angela and we have a baby girl called Carys. In February 2008 I was ordained and inducted into Colston Milton Parish Church in the north of Glasgow.'

Martin Scott is a Church of Scotland minister and has been Secretary of that Church's Ministries Council since 2005. He has previously been a music teacher, a Baptist minister and a theological educator in Manchester, from where he visited Manila as part of a sabbatical leave in 1994.

Richard Sharples is a Methodist Minister and Iona Community member living in Wrexham. He is married to Biddy, with three daughters, Annie, Mary and Eve. They are committed to a green lifestyle and to practical hospitality. Richard is a keen cyclist and allotment holder.

Phil Smith is an ordained deacon in the Anglican Church, serving his title in South Shields.

Clare Speedie lives in Stirling and since February 2009 has worked for the Going Carbon Neutral Stirling project (GCNS). She has a strong interest in social and environmental justice and is happy to be able to bring these issues to people's notice.

Chris Sunderland is a scientist, storyteller, priest and founder of EarthAbbey, a Christian community dedicated to living more in tune with the earth.

Alison Swinfen is a member of the Iona Community, writer and allotment holder. Her first collection of poems *Through Wood* is published by Wild Goose Publications.

Fiona van Wissen – 'I am an outdoor educator who loves exploring nature with young children, in forests, tide pools or even puddles! I am a former volunteer children's worker with the Iona Community and am also involved with L'Arche communities in Canada and Italy.'

Unfortunately it was not possible to obtain biographical details of every contributor.

AUTHOR INDEX

A
A Rocha 211
Rowena Aberdeen 213
Matthew Aitken 147
Judith Allinson 145
Stephen Alliss 185
Hilary Ash 207

B
Chris Baker 158
Marnie Barrell 38, 214, 221
John L Bell 54
Ruth Bell 30
Pat Bennett 23, 66, 87, 132, 155, 182, 194, 218
Briggs, Anna 185
Ruth Burgess 37, 53, 88, 98, 153, 200

C
Sonia Christie 173
Ruth Conway 204
Joanna, Emily and Sam Crawshaw 58
Biddy Crossfield 163

D
Christine Davidson 84, 174
Michael Davidson 36
Simon Davis 82, 94, 142, 167, 195
Barry Dickinson 30
Jill Duffield 202

E
Eco-congregation 52, 68, 218
Stuart Elliott 138, 141, 154, 176, 178, 196, 201

G
Ian Galloway 54
Kathy Galloway 38, 54, 60, 205
Timothy Gorringe 225
Jenny Gregory 181, 216

H
Roddy Hamilton 30, 50, 51, 52, 73, 77
Eleanor Harris 21, 42, 154, 162, 199, 215, 216

I
Iona Abbey Worship Book 79

WILD GOOSE PUBLICATIONS IS PART OF THE IONA COMMUNITY:

- An ecumenical movement of men and women from different walks of life and different traditions in the Christian church
- Committed to the gospel of Jesus Christ, and to following where that leads, even into the unknown
- Engaged together, and with people of goodwill across the world, in acting, reflecting and praying for justice, peace and the integrity of creation
- Convinced that the inclusive community we seek must be embodied in the community we practise

Together with our staff, we are responsible for:

- Our islands residential centres of Iona Abbey, the MacLeod Centre on Iona, and Camas Adventure Centre on the Ross of Mull

and in Glasgow:

- The administration of the Community
- Our work with young people
- Our publishing house, Wild Goose Publications
- Our association in the revitalising of worship with the Wild Goose Resource Group

The Iona Community was founded in Glasgow in 1938 by George MacLeod, minister, visionary and prophetic witness for peace, in the context of the poverty and despair of the Depression. Its original task of rebuilding the monastic ruins of Iona Abbey became a sign of hopeful rebuilding of community in Scotland and beyond. Today, we are about 250 members, mostly in Britain, and 1500 associate members, with 1400 friends worldwide. Together and apart, 'we follow the light we have, and pray for more light'.

For information on the Iona Community contact:
The Iona Community, Fourth Floor, Savoy House, 140 Sauchiehall Street,
Glasgow G2 3DH, UK. Phone: 0141 332 6343
e-mail: admin@iona.org.uk; web: www.iona.org.uk

For enquiries about visiting Iona, please contact:
Iona Abbey, Isle of Iona, Argyll PA76 6SN, UK. Phone: 01681 700404
e-mail: ionacomm@iona.org.uk